Universal credit
What you need
to know

The University of Law

2 New York Street
Manchester
M1 4HJ

Child Poverty Action Group

Published by the Child Poverty Action Group
94 White Lion Street
London N1 9PF
Tel: 020 7837 7979
staff@cpag.org.uk
www.cpag.org.uk
© Child Poverty Action Group 2013

A CIP record for this book is available from the British Library.
ISBN: 978 1 906076 72 6

Child Poverty Action Group is a charity registered in England and Wales (registration
number 294841) and in Scotland (registration number SC039339), and is a company
limited by guarantee, registered in England (registration number 1993854). VAT number:
690 808117

Cover and typography by Devious Designs
Content management system by KonnectSoft
Typeset by David Lewis XML Associates Ltd
Printed and bound by CPI Group (UK) Ltd, Croydon, CR0 4YY

Authors
The authors of this book are all welfare rights workers at CPAG in Scotland.
Alison Gillies is a welfare rights worker with the Children and Families project.
Henri Krishna is a welfare rights worker with the BME Communities project.
Judith Paterson is welfare rights co-ordinator.
Jon Shaw is a welfare rights worker with the Children and Families project.
Angela Toal is a welfare rights worker with the Benefits for Students project.
Mark Willis is a welfare rights worker with the Tax Credits and Early Years project.

Acknowledgements
Many thanks are due to Nicola Johnston for her efficient and thorough editing and for managing the production. Thanks are also due to Katherine Dawson for producing the index and Kathleen Armstrong for proofreading the text. We are also particularly grateful for all the hard work done by Nigel Taylor of Devious Designs and Mike Hatt of DLXML. The authors would like to thank Pauline Chalmers, Lorraine Murphy and Anna Carr for their invaluable support, and acknowledge David Simmons' contribution to the first edition of this guide.

About Child Poverty Action Group

Child Poverty Action Group is a national charity working for the abolition of child poverty in the UK and for the improvement of the lives of low-income families.

To help achieve this goal, we have developed a high level of expertise in the welfare benefits system. We use this to support thousands of frontline advisers with our expert training and free helplines, enabling them to give families the best information and advice.

We also publish a widely used series of practitioner handbooks: our annual *Welfare Benefits and Tax Credits Handbook* (known as 'the adviser's bible') is used by Citizens Advice Bureaux, local authorities and law centres throughout the UK.

Our policy, campaigning and lobbying work builds support for policy improvements to help children living in poverty. We host the End Child Poverty campaign, a national coalition of charities, faith groups and other organisations working to hold the government to its target of beating child poverty by 2020.

If you would like to help with our campaign to end child poverty, please visit our website at www.cpag.org.uk. You can also get the latest news by following us on Facebook (www.facebook.com/cpaguk) and Twitter @CPAGUK.

Keeping up to date

Advisers can get the latest information on universal credit by booking on a CPAG training course. We can also provide your workplace with in-house training. See www.cpag.org.uk/training for more information.

Our *Welfare Benefits and Tax Credits Handbook* 2013/14, published in April 2013, contains the latest information on universal credit, personal independence payment and other welfare reform measures. It also tells you all you need to know about entitlement to benefits and tax credits from April 2013.

Getting advice

Your local Citizens Advice Bureau or other advice centre can give you advice and support on benefits. See www.citizensadvice.org.uk if you live in England or Wales, or www.cas.org.uk if you live in Scotland.

CPAG has an advice line for advisers.

For advisers in England and Wales:
Telephone: 020 7833 4627, Monday to Thursday 2pm to 4pm, Friday 10am to 12pm

For advisers in Scotland:
Telephone: 0141 552 0552, Monday to Friday 10am to 12pm
Email: advice@cpagscotland.org.uk

Contents

Chapter 1
Introduction

This chapter covers:

1. What is universal credit?

2. What has happened to the old system?

3. How is universal credit administered?

4. How is universal credit different?

What you need to know

- Universal credit is a new benefit for people of working age who are in or out of work. It is being introduced in stages from October 2013.

- Universal credit is administered by the Department for Work and Pensions, with the majority of contact with claimants online.

- The amount of your universal credit depends on your income and savings – ie, it is 'means tested'. You do not need to have paid national insurance contributions to qualify.

- Other means-tested benefits and tax credits are being abolished. Claimants are being transferred from the old system to universal credit over several years.

- Some other benefits remain outside universal credit, but are also being reformed.

- The Welfare Reform Act 2012 contains the basic provisions for universal credit. More details are set out in regulations.

1. What is universal credit?

Universal credit is a social security benefit for people of working age, being introduced in stages throughout Great Britain from October 2013. It combines means-tested support for adults, children and housing costs into one benefit. The existing working-age means-tested benefits and tax credits are being abolished. This means that if you are a lone parent, sick or disabled, a carer, unemployed, or in low-paid work and need help with living expenses, including your rent or mortgage, the means-tested benefit you claim is universal credit.

The guiding principles of universal credit are simplicity and making work pay. Claiming one benefit whether in or out of work, and in different circumstances, is intended to increase take-up and reduce problems of fraud and error due to complexity. The success or otherwise of universal credit depends on the availability of jobs, and that people should always be able to see that they are better off in work, whatever they earn. Universal credit is designed to increase 'digital inclusion' by being primarily accessed online, and to promote 'financial capability' by normally being paid monthly.

What does this guide cover?

The first edition of this guide was published shortly after the Welfare Reform Act was passed on 8 March 2012, providing an overview of the basic principles of universal credit. This second edition is informed by detailed regulations and further guidance from the Department for Work and Pensions issued up to July 2013, after the first pilot began. Some of the original plans outlined in 2012 have been dropped or altered. This guide tells you what you need to know about universal credit, including who can claim and how it works.

The basic facts you need to know are listed at the start of each chapter. There is a glossary of common terms in the appendix.

2. What has happened to the old system?

The old social security system is not going away for some years yet, and is not being fully replaced. Working-age means-tested benefits and tax credits are being abolished and replaced with universal credit.

What the law says

Benefits and tax credits being abolished

The benefits and tax credits being abolished and replaced by universal credit are:
- income support
- income-based jobseeker's allowance
- income-related employment and support allowance
- housing benefit
- child tax credit
- working tax credit

Section 33 Welfare Reform Act 2012

The benefits are being abolished for new claims as universal credit begins to be introduced from October 2013. Under current plans, no new claims for tax credits can be accepted from people of working age after 6 April 2014.

If you are already getting one of the benefits or tax credits that are being abolished in October 2013, payments do not stop immediately. There is a period of transfer during which you continue to get these benefits or tax credits until you are moved onto universal credit. There is more about the transfer to universal credit in Chapter 8.

Universal credit does not replace all current benefits, however, and it is not a single working-age benefit system. You can still claim the benefits in Box A after universal credit has been introduced, although some are being reformed.

Council tax benefit has been abolished, and is not part of universal credit. Instead, local authorities and the Scottish and Welsh governments have responsibility for council tax reduction schemes from April 2013, with (in most areas) a 10 per cent cut in the budget.

Crisis loans and community care grants from the social fund have also been abolished and replaced by schemes devised and delivered by local authorities and the Scottish and Welsh governments.

Box A

Which benefits remain?
- attendance allowance
- bereavement allowance
- bereavement payment
- carer's allowance
- child benefit
- cold weather payments
- constant attendance allowance
- disability living allowance
- contributory employment and support allowance
- free school lunches
- funeral payments
- guardian's allowance
- Healthy Start vouchers
- help with health costs
- industrial injuries benefits
- contribution-based jobseeker's allowance
- maternity allowance
- pension credit
- personal independence payment
- retirement pension
- school clothing grant
- statutory adoption pay
- statutory maternity pay
- statutory paternity pay
- statutory sick pay
- Sure Start maternity grant
- war disablement pension
- war widow's and widower's pension
- widowed parent's allowance
- winter fuel payment

3. How is universal credit administered?

The **Department for Work and Pensions (DWP)** is the sole government agency responsible for the administration of universal credit. The DWP also deals with the out-of-work benefits that are being abolished and handles the transfer of these claims to universal credit. Different sections within the DWP deal with most of the other benefits that remain outside of universal credit, but still interact with it. This includes contributory benefits, pensions, disability and carer benefits, which are also subject to separate reform.

HM Revenue and Customs (HMRC) administers tax credits, which are being abolished. However, child benefit remains the responsibility of HMRC and is still a vital part of family incomes, whether receiving universal credit or not. HMRC receives 'real-time information' on earnings from employers which is then accessed by the DWP so that universal credit payments can be automatically adjusted as earnings change.

Local authorities currently administer housing benefit, which is being abolished, although existing claims continue until they are transferred to universal credit, which is planned to happen by the end of 2017. Local authorities continue to deal with housing benefit for older people and housing costs for people in certain types of supported accommodation, and retain rent officers' functions in the private sector. They are also responsible for council tax reduction schemes, discretionary housing payments, grants and other financial help.

'Welfare-to-work' agencies have a key role in the administration of universal credit. Decisions on entitlement, amounts and sanctions are made by a decision maker at the DWP. However, what you have to do in return for universal credit, known as your 'work-related requirements', may be dealt with by other agencies, who act under a contract on behalf of the DWP. These agencies employ personal advisers, who set the terms of your 'claimant commitment', hold 'work-focused interviews' and require you to take particular action to prepare for or search for work. There is more information about the claimant commitment and work-related requirements in Chapter 5.

The role of IT

The government is clear that the ideal process for claiming universal credit is 'digital by default'. It sees this as a necessary part of making claimants ready for work in a world where a sizeable proportion of employment opportunities are accessed online and involve computer skills. This is part of a wider policy of 'digital inclusion' to promote access to the internet for all sections of the community so they can take advantage of the information, services and better deals available online. The government has acknowledged that this is not suitable for everyone and there is a need for an alternative for those who cannot manage online, as well as resources for those who need equipment, training or improved broadband coverage to get online.

4. How is universal credit different?

Universal credit is said to be 'a radical new approach'. But how different is it really? Universal credit is not being introduced all at once from October 2013, and the old system will remain in place to some extent for a further four years. It replaces some old benefits, but is not an entirely new start, as much of the detail is similar to the system that has been developed and reformed repeatedly over the last 65 years. For example, most of the rules about how savings and capital are treated are based on the rules for means-tested benefits, and rules that exclude certain groups based on residence or immigration status are very similar. At the same time, a substantial number of old benefits remain in place, outside of universal credit.

Monthly assessment and payment periods

Universal credit is assessed according to circumstances over a calendar month. Awards are calculated according to earnings and other income received in a month, and payment is made in one monthly sum. This presents a challenge for claimants who are on weekly or four-weekly wages, or who may be used to budgeting with fortnightly payments of adult benefits, and separate, four-weekly payments of child tax credit.

Online access

Universal credit is claimed online, with telephone access in limited circumstances and face-to-face assistance in exceptional cases. There is no paper claim form.

Abolition of hours rules

The old benefits and tax credits system has a variety of rules that make a difference to entitlement and the amount received, depending on whether the you or your partner work less or more than 16, 24 or 30 hours a week. Under universal credit, all work is permitted, encouraged, and in some cases, compulsory, while earnings are automatically taken into account.

Work incentives

Universal credit involves an additional £2.3 billion increase in expenditure, particularly for people who are in work, by allowing them to keep more of their universal credit as earnings rise. These incentives are most generous for people who have no housing costs, and make the biggest difference, in comparison to the old system, to people who work a few hours a week, encouraging claimants to take on 'mini jobs', for which childcare support is also available for the first time.

What CPAG says

Work incentives

The universal credit system does not give people any more money if they are out of work, and in many cases, such as for some under 25s, most disabled children and severely disabled adults, it allows less to live on. Even in work some groups may be worse off, or find incentives are not so generous, when compared to the various threads of the old system.

In-work conditionality

Universal credit claimants who work part time are obliged to look for more work. This was never a feature of the working tax credit system, in which reaching a certain level of hours was sufficient to qualify, although there was an added incentive to reach 30 hours a week. In a world where temporary jobs, agency work and fluctuating hours are common, universal credit claimants may be sanctioned if they cannot do enough to increase hours or pay.

Box B

Welfare reforms remaining part of universal credit

Universal credit is being introduced after unprecedented cuts in the social security budget amounting to £22 billion a year by 2014/15. Significantly, many of the most damaging cuts remain an integral part of universal credit.

The **'bedroom tax'** restricts the help with rent for people of working age in social rented housing if they are deemed to have a 'spare' bedroom. The assessment of need, which allows one bedroom for two children under 10, or of the same sex, is the same for the calculation of help with rent in universal credit. This affects many families with children who do not realise they have a 'spare' bedroom because a child is sleeping in it, and disabled people who need an additional room for a variety of reasons.

The **benefit cap** is extended under universal credit. Before the introduction of universal credit, any reduction due to the cap was applied to housing benefit. Families not receiving housing benefit, including owner occupiers getting help with mortgage interest, were less affected by the cap. Under universal credit, the reduction is applied to the total received, including families not liable for rent or who get support with mortgage interest.

Recent cuts to **local housing allowance** mean that only three out of 10 private-rented properties in a 'broad area' are affordable if you rely on housing benefit to help you pay your rent, including if you are in work. This is replicated under universal credit, leaving many private tenants with a shortfall, or together with

---

the above changes, looking to move to cheaper areas, possibly far away from schools, family, friends and work.

The **work capability assessment**, used for employment and support allowance to decide 'limited capability for work', is not going away. It has been criticised as flawed by an independent review, and has seen the number of appeals more than double. The work capability assessment determines how much a sick or disabled person can receive in universal credit, and what s/he is required to do to prepare for work.

What CPAG says

The legacy of the cuts

Box B lists just a few of the 42 separate cuts that have put low-income families under increasing pressure in recent years. Universal credit is also subject to the lock of 1 per cent on annual uprating of main benefit amounts in 2014/15 and 2015/16, a cut in real terms. Analysis for CPAG in March 2013 found that there is likely to be an increase of 600,000 children in absolute poverty by 2015, on the basis of welfare reform policies from 2010 to 2015, and after any projected reduction in child poverty due to universal credit.

For a 'once in a generation' reform, universal credit looks increasingly like a missed opportunity, especially when considering the negligible impact on the rising tide of child poverty. The Institute for Fiscal Studies predicted a growth in child poverty of 1.1 million by 2020 due to the recession and welfare reform. The government's original estimate of 350,000 children lifted out of poverty by universal credit is decidedly unambitious and has already been downgraded. Without progressive investment in jobs and people, universal credit is nowhere near enough to meet the commitment in the Child Poverty Act to end child poverty by 2020.

Chapter 2
Who can get universal credit

This chapter covers:

1. Who can get universal credit?

2. What are the basic rules?

3. What are the financial conditions?

4. Who cannot get universal credit?

What you need to know

- To get universal credit, you must meet the basic rules of entitlement and the financial conditions.

- There are basic rules about your age, residence in Great Britain, whether you are in education and about agreeing to a 'claimant commitment', which is a kind of contract between you and the Department for Work and Pensions.

- The financial conditions are about your income and capital – eg, savings, investments and certain types of property. You cannot get universal credit if your capital is above £16,000 (although some capital is ignored). The amount of universal credit you get depends on the level of your income compared with the maximum universal credit for someone in your circumstances.

- If you are in a couple, you make a joint claim. Usually, both of you must meet the basic rules and the financial conditions.

1. Who can get universal credit?

Universal credit is a benefit for both single people and couples on a low income to provide financial support for living costs, children, housing costs and other needs. You can get universal credit if you are in or out of work.

You are eligible for universal credit if you meet the basic rules of entitlement and the financial conditions. Provided you meet these conditions, you are eligible for universal credit regardless of your particular circumstances. For example, you can claim if you are:

- a parent, including a lone parent
- ill or disabled
- a carer
- unemployed
- employed or self-employed

EXAMPLES

Who can get universal credit

George has been made redundant. Depending on his income and his other circumstances, he can get universal credit to provide him with some financial help.

Rosie is a lone parent working 12 hours a week in a low-paid job. One of her children is disabled, and they live in a housing association property. She can claim universal credit to provide her with some financial help.

Your specific circumstances are taken into account to decide how much universal credit you get, and to decide what you are expected to do to move towards work.

There is more information in Chapter 3 on the amount of universal credit you can get, and in Chapter 5 on the 'work-related requirements' you may need to satisfy.

Couples

If you are in a couple, you normally make a joint claim with your partner. Both of you must normally satisfy the basic rules of entitlement, and you must meet the financial conditions.

You count as a member of a couple if you are living together and you are married, or if you are living together as if you were married. If you are both of the same sex, you count as a couple if you are living together and you are civil partners, or if you are living together as if you were civil partners. In some circumstances, you have to claim as a single person even though you are a member of a couple – eg, you usually have to claim as a single person if your partner is under 18 but you are not.

There is more information about these rules in Chapter 4.

In some circumstances, it is possible to get universal credit as a couple even though one of you does not meet the basic rules. This applies if one of you:

- has reached pension credit age and the other has not
- is in education and the other is not

EXAMPLE

One member of a couple is in education

Joan is on a full-time undergraduate course and her partner Mike is unemployed. They have no children. They can claim universal credit as a couple even though Joan is in education.

If you are a couple and your partner has not accepted a 'claimant commitment' but you have, you cannot get universal credit. You must each accept your own claimant commitment to qualify for universal credit if you are a couple.

See Chapter 5 for more information about the claimant commitment.

2. What are the basic rules?

To be entitled to universal credit, you must meet the basic rules and also meet the financial conditions. There are some exceptions to the basic rules which are explained below.

What the law says

The basic rules

You meet the basic rules for universal credit if you:
- are aged 18 or over
- are under the qualifying age for pension credit
- are not in education
- are in Great Britain
- accept a claimant commitment

There are some exceptions to these basic rules.

Section 4 Welfare Reform Act 2012

Your age

If you are under 18

Usually, you must be aged 18 or over to claim universal credit but you can claim at age 16 or 17 if you:

- have a child
- have a disability and get disability living allowance or personal independence payment and have 'limited capability for work'
- are 'without parental support'

If you claim for yourself, it will mean that your parent cannot continue to claim for you so it may be important to check this before you claim.

If you are *not* a 'student' (see page 15) at school or college you can also get universal credit if you:

- are pregnant and the baby is due in 11 weeks or sooner
- are ill or disabled and have 'limited capability for work' but you do not need to have another disability benefit
- are a carer – usually you must also get carer's allowance which is another benefit for carers who look after someone with a disability

If you are a care leaver aged 16 or 17, you can only get universal credit if you have a child, or are ill or disabled but it does not include any 'housing element' for your housing costs.

What the law says

Who is without parental support?

You are 'without parental support' if you are living away from your parents because you are estranged from them or because there is a risk to your health, or your parents cannot support you because they are ill, disabled, in prison or not allowed to enter Great Britain, or you are an orphan. This will not apply to you if you are looked after by the local authority or somebody else (such as a grandparent) is acting in place of a parent.

Regulation 8(3) The Universal Credit Regulations 2013

If you are over pension credit age

To get universal credit, you must be below the qualifying age for pension credit. This is gradually increasing from age 60 and, under current plans, will reach 66 in 2020. If you are in a couple and one of you is over the qualifying age for pension credit, you are eligible for universal credit and cannot choose to claim pension credit instead. If one of you is under and the other is over the qualifying age for pension credit and you already get pension credit, you stay on pension credit and do not have to claim universal credit.

EXAMPLE

One member of a couple is over pension credit age

Charlie is 64 and his wife Joan is 58. They can get universal credit. Even though Charlie is over the qualifying age for pension credit, they cannot get pension credit.

Joan has to meet work-related requirements as a condition of getting universal credit, but Charlie does not.

If you are in education

In general, you cannot get universal credit if you are 'receiving education' – ie, you are a student. However, there are some exceptions to this, which allow you to claim universal credit even if you are a student.

What the law says

Who is a student?

- From your 16th birthday to 1 September after your 19th birthday, you are a student if you are at school or college on a non-advanced course (eg, below degree or HNC level) or you are in training that is 'approved' by the DWP.

- You are a student while you are on a full-time course of advanced education – eg, at HNC or degree level.

- You are a student while you are on another kind of full-time course, advanced or non-advanced, and you get a loan or grant for your maintenance.

- Even if you are not in one of the three groups above, you count as a student if your course is not compatible with the hours that you are expected to be available for work or with other work-related requirements you are expected to meet for your universal credit claim. For example, if you are on a full-time non-advanced course and do not get a grant for maintenance, and you are expected to look for full-time work, it is likely that you will count as a student and will therefore not be able to get universal credit (unless you are in one of the exception groups outlined below).

Regulations 5, 12 and 13 The Universal Credit Regulations 2013

Which students can get universal credit?

You can get universal credit while you are student if you are in one (or more) of the following groups.

- You have a child.

- You are a single foster parent (this includes some kinship carers).
- You are disabled and get disability living allowance or personal independence payment and you have been assessed as having 'limited capability for work' (there is more about this assessment in Chapter 3).
- You are aged under 22 'without parental support' on a non-advanced course which you started before your 21st birthday.
- You are a member of a couple and your partner is not a student.
- You have taken time out from your course because of illness or caring responsibilities, have now recovered or the caring responsibilities have ended, and you are waiting to rejoin your course.
- You are over the qualifying age for pension credit.

How much you get, if any, depends on your income. Student loans and some grants count as income, but usually only during the academic year.

EXAMPLE

Students who can get universal credit

Graham is on a full-time advanced course. He is disabled and gets disability living allowance, and has limited capability for work. He can claim universal credit.

Lauren is on a full-time advanced course and is a lone parent. She can claim universal credit.

In each case, whether they get any universal credit or not will depend on what other income they have.

Residence in Great Britain

In general, you must be in Great Britain to claim universal credit, although there are exceptions to this.

Are you going abroad?

You can continue to get universal credit if you are abroad for up to one month. There are only limited circumstances when you can get it for longer than this – eg, for up to two months if a close relative has died or up to six months if the trip is to get medical treatment. For a couple, if you stay at home and your partner is abroad for longer than a month, your universal credit will normally go down, so it is important to tell the DWP. Some people who work abroad can get universal credit – eg, members of the armed forces.

Have you come to Great Britain from abroad?

In some cases, even though you are in Great Britain, you cannot get universal credit. This mostly applies to people coming from abroad, as the following rules explain.

There is a rule about immigration status. You cannot get universal credit if you are a 'person subject to immigration control' (although there are some exceptions). You will usually have 'no recourse to public funds' stamped on your passport, which means you cannot claim universal credit (or most other benefits). If you have refugee leave, humanitarian protection or discretionary leave and in some other circumstances, you can get universal credit.

There is also a rule about residence in Great Britain. You must have a 'right to reside' in Great Britain. If you are a UK national, you have a right to reside. This rule mostly affects nationals of countries in the European Economic Area. In most cases, if you are working or looking for work (ie, you meet all 'work-related requirements' for universal credit), you have a right to reside. There are other circumstances in which you may also have a right to reside.

You may also have to be 'habitually resident' before you can get universal credit. This means, very generally, that you have been living here for a while and intend to stay for some time to come. Usually, if you have a 'right to reside' you do not also have to show that you are habitually resident.

EXAMPLES

Right to reside for universal credit

Natasha is French and a lone parent. She is working full-time in Great Britain. She has a right to reside as a worker and can claim universal credit.

Saskia is Lithuanian and a lone parent with a six-month-old baby. She is a full-time student, but has never worked in Great Britain. She does not have a right to reside and cannot claim universal credit.

Accepting a claimant commitment

To be entitled to universal credit, you must normally accept a 'claimant commitment'. This sets out what you must do to receive your universal credit award. The key part of a claimant commitment is about 'work-related requirements'.

There is more information about the claimant commitment in Chapter 5.

EXAMPLE

The basic rules

Jane and Kevin are a couple, both aged 20. They are UK nationals and live in London. Neither are in education. They want to know if they can claim universal credit.

They are within the age conditions, they are in Great Britain, and they are not in education, so they can claim universal credit. They must claim jointly as a couple. They must also meet the financial conditions and agree to meet certain requirements as part of their claimant commitment.

Their income must then be compared with the maximum amount of universal credit for their circumstances to see if they get an award of universal credit and, if so, how much this will be.

3. What are the financial conditions?

To be entitled to universal credit, your income must be low enough. How much income you can have and still be entitled to some universal credit depends on your circumstances. Usually, as your income goes up the amount of universal credit you get goes down. If you have a partner, it is your combined income that counts. Your capital (eg, savings and investments) must not be more than £16,000. If it is higher than £16,000, you are not entitled to universal credit. If you have a partner, it is your combined capital that counts.

You must also meet the basic rules.

There is more information about the income and capital rules in Chapter 3.

4. Who cannot get universal credit?

Universal credit is being introduced gradually, so you can only claim when it has been introduced in your area. If you already get income support, income-based jobseeker's allowance, income-related employment and support allowance, housing benefit, child tax credit or working tax credit, you cannot get universal credit until your benefit is transferred. There is more about moving to universal credit in Chapter 8.

If you are in prison, you can get universal credit for up to six months but only for your housing costs (the 'housing costs element').

You cannot get universal credit if you are a member of a religious order and fully maintained by the order.

What CPAG says

Who can claim

Universal credit is a single benefit with one set of rules. In deciding what these rules should be, the government has selected from the existing benefits that are being replaced. It has been suggested that in some respects the government has 'chosen the least favourable option that currently exists and [has] decided to apply it universally'. This concern runs through many of the entitlement conditions for universal credit.

- Tax credits have no capital limit while other means-tested benefits do have a limit. Under universal credit, the capital limit applies to everyone, penalising savers. Someone with over £16,000 savings, but no other income, would have got child tax credit to help with the costs of her/his children. The same person claiming universal credit would get nothing, although there is some protection for existing claimants.

- Most benefits have a lower age limit of 16, although for jobseeker's allowance it is 18. A lower age limit of 18 applies across universal credit, with only a few exceptions. These exceptions restrict entitlement, so some young people are worse off under the new system, particularly 16- and 17-year-olds who need help with rent who under the old system would be eligible for housing benefit.

- Student entitlement to benefits is significantly changed under universal credit. Disabled students are particularly disadvantaged. They can only get universal credit if they have limited capability for work *and* get disability living allowance or personal independence payment. Previous rules were more generous, particularly for help with rent for disabled students.

As a general principle, CPAG supports the idea of benefit simplification, but not if the approach adopted is so broad that many people on low incomes are entitled to less support.

Further information

There is more information about who can get universal credit and other benefits you may qualify for in CPAG's *Welfare Benefits and Tax Credits Handbook*.

Chapter 3
The amount of universal credit

This chapter covers:

1. The maximum amount of universal credit

2. How does your income and capital affect universal credit?

3. How much universal credit do you get?

What you need to know

- Universal credit includes an amount for you and your partner. This is called the 'standard allowance'.

- Amounts for any children (the 'child element') for whom you are responsible are added to the standard allowance.

- The child element is increased if your child is disabled.

- Extra amounts are also added to the standard allowance, depending on your circumstances. There is an additional amount if someone in your family is ill or disabled, provided s/he meets the qualifying conditions. There is also an additional amount if you or your partner are caring for a disabled person. There are also amounts for rent and mortgage costs, and for childcare costs.

- If you have other income, this reduces the amount of universal credit to which you are entitled, although some income is ignored.

- You are not entitled to universal credit if you have more than £16,000 in capital.

1. The maximum amount of universal credit

Universal credit is a 'means-tested' benefit. This means that the amount you get depends on your family circumstances and on how much other income (if any) you have. As your income increases, the amount of your universal credit award reduces.

Your maximum universal credit is made up of the total of:

- a 'standard allowance'
- a 'child element' for each child
- an amount for each disabled child (at a lower or higher rate)
- an amount for an ill or disabled adult (at a lower or higher rate)
- a 'carer element' if you or your partner care for a disabled person
- a 'housing costs element'
- a 'childcare costs element'

Each of these amounts has its own qualifying conditions. The rest of this section explains when these amounts apply and how your maximum amount of universal credit is worked out. There are examples at the end of the section. If you have no income or your income is below a certain level, maximum universal credit is the amount you get.

Amount for you and your family

Universal credit includes an amount for you, your partner and any children you have. The amount for you and your partner (if you have one) is called the 'standard allowance'. How much you get depends on whether you are making a single claim or a joint claim and whether you are aged under 25.

Standard allowance rates per month	
Single claimant under 25	£246.81
Single claimant 25 or over	£311.55
Joint claimants both under 25	£387.42
Joint claimants where at least one is 25 or over	£489.06

If you are responsible for any children, your universal credit includes an additional amount (called the 'child element') for each child under 16 and for each young person who is 16 to 18 (or 19 in some cases) and, for example, is still at school or college on a non-advanced course.

Child element rates per month	
Eldest or only child or qualifying young person	£272.08
Each other child or qualifying young person	£226.67

Only one claimant (a single person or a couple) can claim for a particular child. If a child normally lives with more than one person (eg, separated parents), the person with the 'main responsibility' for the child can claim universal credit for her/him.

Additional amount if your child is disabled

If your child is disabled, your universal credit includes an extra amount. There are two different levels of payment depending on the severity of your child's disability.

- You get the lower amount if your child gets disability living allowance or, if s/he is aged 16 or over, personal independence payment.

- You get the higher amount if your child gets disability living allowance highest rate care component, personal independence payment enhanced rate daily living component, or is registered or certified blind.

Amounts for a disabled child per month	
Lower amount	£123.62
Higher amount	£352.92

Additional amount if you or your partner are ill or disabled

If you or your partner are ill or disabled, you may get an additional amount added to your standard allowance. There are two levels of this additional amount, reflecting the severity of your difficulties: a lower amount if you have 'limited capability for work' (see Box A); and a higher amount if you have 'limited capability for work and work-related activity' (see Box B).

Box A
Limited capability for work test

'Limited capability for work' is a test of whether your health problems or disabilities mean that you are currently unable to work. It is also used to decide whether you qualify for employment and support allowance. The assessment normally involves you filling in a questionnaire and attending a medical examination. You are likely to be assessed regularly to check whether you still meet these conditions. If you do not return the questionnaire about your health problems or do not attend the medical without good reason, you are likely to be treated as not satisfying the conditions. If you get employment and support allowance, you do not need to have a separate assessment for universal credit.

Box B
Limited capability for work and work-related activity test

The severity of your health problems is decided by looking at whether or not you have a 'limited capability for work and work-related activity'. This test is designed to identify whether your illness or disability is so serious that, currently, you should not be expected to think about returning to work. You may be regularly assessed to check whether you still meet these conditions. If you get employment and support allowance, you will not need to have a separate assessment for universal credit.

In some circumstances, you are treated as having limited capability for work without having to go through this assessment. For example, this applies if you are a hospital inpatient (the DWP can extend it when you leave hospital until you have recovered) or you are in residential rehabilitation for drug or alcohol problems. It also applies if you are at least pension credit age and get disability living allowance or personal independence payment.

In some circumstances, you are treated as having limited capability for work and work-related activity without having to go through the assessment. For example, this applies if you are terminally ill or you are having chemotherapy or radiotherapy for cancer, or are likely to do so in the next six months, or are recovering from this treatment. It also applies if you are at least pension credit age and get attendance allowance, disability living allowance highest rate care component or personal independence payment enhanced rate daily living component

Amounts for ill health or disability per month	
Limited capability for work element	£123.62
Limited capability for work and work-related activity element	£303.66

There is usually a waiting period before you get either of these elements. The waiting period is normally at least three months. If you are are terminally ill, there is no waiting period.

If both you and your partner have limited capability for work and/or work-related activity, you only get one element. You get the higher element that applies. You cannot get the limited capability for work element or the limited capability for work and work-related activity element in addition to the carer element. You get the highest one that applies. However, if you are in a couple, one of you can qualify for this element and the other can qualify for the carer element.

If you are getting either the limited capability for work or limited capability for work and work-related activity element and you start work, you do not automatically lose the element, but your capability may be reassessed. If you are already in work and your weekly earnings are at least 16 times the national minimum wage, you can only be newly assessed to get these elements if you get disability living allowance, personal independence payment or attendance allowance.

EXAMPLE

Couple, one is ill and the other a carer

Tom has cancer and is recovering from chemotherapy. Barbara is looking after him. Tom gets personal independence payment. Their universal credit includes a limited capability for work and work-related activity element of £303.66 and a carer element of £144.70 a month.

Additional amount if you or your partner are a carer

If you are caring for someone who is severely disabled, you may get an additional amount added to your standard allowance. This is called the 'carer element' and is £144.70 per month.

You can get the carer element if you have 'regular and substantial' caring responsibilities for a severely disabled person. The person you care for must get attendance allowance, disability living allowance care component middle or highest rate, or personal independence payment daily living component (either rate). The easiest way to qualify is to claim carer's allowance, which is another benefit for carers. But even if you do not get this benefit, you can still get the carer element if you care for the person for at least 35 hours a week. Only one claimant can get the carer element for a disabled person, even though more than one person may be caring for that person.

Amount for housing costs

Universal credit includes an amount for certain housing costs. This is called the 'housing costs element'. The housing costs element can cover rent, mortgage interest and some service charges. The housing costs element will usually only cover the housing costs for the home you live in. However, in certain situations, it can be paid for a home you are not living in. For example, if you are prevented from moving into a new home because you are waiting for disability adaptations to be carried out, the housing costs element can be included for up to one month before you actually move in.

There are also limited situations in which you can receive a housing costs element on two homes. For example, if you are disabled and you are waiting for a new home to be adapted, the housing costs element can be paid on two homes for up to one month. If you are fleeing domestic violence, living in temporary accommodation and intending to return home, the housing costs element can be paid on both homes for up to 12 months.

Sometimes, although you do live in the house, you will not be able to get the housing costs element. For example, you cannot get the housing costs element if you are paying rent to a close relative and you are also living with her/him.

Help with rent

The amount you get to help you with your rent depends on how many people are in your family and on your circumstances.

If you are renting from a **local authority or housing association**, the amount of the housing costs element is usually the same as the rent you pay, plus certain service charges. However, the amount may be limited if you are considered to be living in a property that is too big for you – see Box C for how many bedrooms you are allowed. The rules may be different if you are in temporary accommodation because you are homeless.

If you rent from a **private landlord**, the amount of the housing costs element is limited to the 'local housing allowance' in your area for the size of property you are assessed as needing (the local housing allowance reflects the lowest one-third of market rents available).

The number of bedrooms you are allowed is the same as in Box C except that the most you are allowed is four. There is a different rule if you are single, aged under 35 and have no dependants. In this situation, with some exceptions, you are only eligible for a housing costs element to cover the rent for a room in shared accommodation. You can check the local housing allowance that applies to you at www.gov.uk.

Box C

How many bedrooms are you allowed if you rent from a local authority or housing association?

You are allowed one bedroom for each of the following:

- a couple
- a person who is aged 16 or over
- two children of the same sex
- two children who are under 10
- any other child
- one extra room if you have a carer (or carers) providing overnight care to a disabled person

You may be allowed an additional bedroom if, for example, you have a child with a disability or you are a foster carer.

If you have one more bedroom than you are allowed, your housing costs element is reduced by 14 per cent of your rent. If you have two or more extra bedrooms, your housing costs element is reduced by 25 per cent of your rent.

EXAMPLE

Housing costs element

Tess is a lone parent with two children – a boy and a girl aged 10 and 12. She is allowed three bedrooms under universal credit rules. Her housing association house has four bedrooms and her monthly rent is £400. Her housing costs element is reduced by 14 per cent of her rent (£56). Her housing costs element is £344 (£400 minus £56).

The amount of housing costs element you get for help with rent (whether you rent from a local authority, housing association or private landlord) is reduced if you have any 'non-dependants' living with you. A non-dependant is someone like an adult son or daughter, or a relative, who shares your home. The amount of each 'housing cost contribution' is £68 a month. This is a set rate applied even if you do not actually get any contribution from the non-dependant. However, there are various situations in which no housing cost contribution is deducted. For example, if you or the non-dependant are getting disability living allowance middle or highest rate care component, or personal independence payment daily living component, or if the non-dependant is under 21, there is no housing costs contribution.

Help with mortgage interest

If you are an owner-occupier, you may get help with mortgage interest and with certain service charges. However, you do **not** get help if you are doing any paid work, no matter how few hours.

You do not normally get any help with housing costs during the first three months of your claim for universal credit, although you may be able to get help earlier if you are already on contributory employment and support allowance or contribution-based jobseeker's allowance before getting universal credit. Also, if the housing costs element has stopped being included in your universal credit (eg, because you have started work), you have to wait three months after stopping work before it can be included again.

The amount of your housing costs element is not based on what you actually pay but is calculated by using a standard interest rate. The maximum amount of loan that the housing costs element can be paid for is £200,000. Service charges are also included in the housing costs element.

Amount for childcare costs

You are entitled to the 'childcare costs element' if you are in paid work and you are paying for 'formal' childcare such as a registered childminder, nursery or after-school club.

You can get the childcare costs element if you have a dependent child (up to 1 September after her/his 16th birthday), you are paying for childcare for her/him and you are:

- a lone parent
- a couple and you are both working
- a couple and one of you is working and the other has limited capability for work (see Box A), is caring for a disabled person, or is temporarily away from home

You are treated as working if you are getting statutory sick pay, maternity allowance or statutory maternity, paternity or adoption pay.

You can get childcare costs no matter how few hours you are working. However, the childcare costs must be necessary to enable you to to take up, or continue in, paid work or enable you to maintain childcare arrangements allowing you to return to work – eg, after maternity leave.

The childcare costs element is 70 per cent of your actual childcare costs, up to a maximum of £532.29 a month for one child and £912.50 for two or more children.

What CPAG says

Childcare costs

CPAG is concerned that the proposed provision for childcare costs will make work much less affordable for many parents. Previous rules allowing childcare costs to be disregarded for housing benefit and council tax benefit meant that, in practice, many parents were able to recoup up to 95.5 per cent of their childcare costs. A reduction to 70 per cent therefore represents a significant increase in their childcare outgoings. This development takes place at a time when the cost of childcare is rising significantly. Instead of more parents entering work, we may see more parents leaving work because the childcare that enables them to work is no longer sufficiently affordable to make them better off.

EXAMPLE

Childcare costs

Amara is a lone parent with one child. She is working and has childcare costs of £600 a month. Amara gets £420 a month childcare costs element in her maximum universal credit amount – ie, 70 per cent of £600.

EXAMPLES

Maximum universal credit

Mike and Sharmani are a couple aged 45 and 46 with two children under 10. None of the family have health problems. The couple live in a two-bedroom local authority flat with a monthly rent of £300. They have no childcare costs.

Maximum universal credit
Standard allowance £489.06

Child element x 2 £498.75

Housing costs element £300.00

Total = £1,287.81

Marcia is a lone parent aged 30 with one child. She lives in a three-bedroom housing association house and her rent is £350 a month. The house has one more bedroom than Marcia is allowed under the universal credit rules so her housing costs element is reduced by 14 per cent of the rent. Marcia's child has a disability and gets disability living allowance lowest rate care component. She has childcare costs of £200 a month.

Maximum universal credit:
Standard allowance £311.55

Child element £272.08

Amount for disabled child £123.62

Housing costs element £301.00

Childcare costs elements £140.00

Total = £1,148.25

2. How does your income and capital affect universal credit?

If you and your partner have any income or capital, your universal credit may be affected. Your income could be your earnings or other income, such as other benefits. Your capital includes savings and some property. As your income increases, the amount of universal credit you get will usually decrease. Income belonging to your children is ignored.

Earnings

Your net earnings from employment or self-employment may affect the amount of universal credit you get. Net earnings means your earnings after tax, national insurance and any contribution to an occupational pension scheme.

Your employer is required to report earnings every time you are paid. This is called 'real-time information'.

If your pay is reported by your employer through real-time information, the employed earnings figure used in the universal credit assessment is taken from the amount in the reports received by the DWP in that assessment period.

If your employer does not report your earnings in time, the DWP may ask you to give this information instead.

The earnings figure used in the universal credit calculation is the amount received in each assessment period. (Universal credit is paid monthly in arrears based on information on the previous month – this is called the 'assessment period'.)

If you are self-employed, you must report your earnings monthly to the DWP. Certain expenses are deducted from receipts into the business – eg, regular costs like rent or wages, purchase of stock and utility bills. Flat-rate deductions are made for some expenses such as mileage.

However, if you are self-employed and on a low income, you may be assumed to have higher earnings than you actually do. Normally, unless you are starting a new business, you are treated as earning at least the national minimum wage for someone of your age for the number of hours the DWP expects you to work (if you are expected to work). However, if you are not working regularly, for example, because there is little work available or you are unwell, this may indicate that you are not in 'gainful self-employment' and should not be treated as having income that you do not have.

Statutory sick pay and statutory maternity, paternity and adoption pay count as earnings.

You can keep a certain amount of your earnings before your universal credit is affected. This is called the 'work allowance'. The level of your work allowance depends on your circumstances (eg, if you are a lone parent or have health problems) and also on whether you have the housing costs element included in your universal credit.

Note: a household can only have one work allowance. You get the highest work allowance to which you are entitled.

Work allowance		
Circumstances	Monthly work allowance if you have housing costs element	Monthly work allowance if you have no housing costs elements
Single person (no children)	£111	£111
Couple (no children)	£111	£111
Couple (with children)	£222	£536
Lone parent	£263	£734
Person with limited capability for work	£192	£647

Work allowances

Jon and Barry are a couple with two children. They have a housing costs element included in their universal credit. Their work allowance is £222.

Uche is single and has no children. She has limited capability for work. She has no housing costs element in her universal credit. Her work allowance is £647.

Ildiko is a lone parent with three children. She has no housing costs element in her universal credit. Her work allowance is £734.

How do your earnings affect universal credit?

Once you have worked out which work allowance applies to you and how much of your earnings count, the maximum universal credit is reduced by a proportion of this figure. This is often called the 'taper' – ie, the rate at which your universal credit will 'taper' away as your earnings increase. The taper is 65 per cent. This means that as your earnings increase above the level of your work allowance, your universal credit will decrease by 65 pence for every extra pound you earn.

There are examples of how this works on pages 39 and 40.

Do you have other income?

Only specified types of income are taken into account for universal credit. For example, the following counts:

- occupational or personal pension income
- certain benefits
- maintenance for you or your spouse or partner, but not child maintenance
- student loans and some grants
- certain insurance payments
- income from an annuity or certain trusts
- income from capital

Disability living allowance, personal independence payment, attendance allowance and child benefit are not taken into account as income.

Income which is taken into account reduces your maximum universal credit pound for pound.

What about income from capital?

Any capital you have may affect your universal credit. 'Capital' includes savings, stocks and shares, property and trusts. Certain types of capital are ignored – eg, property which is your main home, personal injury payments placed in a trust fund, some other compensation payments, and, for at least six months, your former home which you are trying to sell. Any capital owned by your children is ignored.

You are treated as still having capital if you deliberately get rid of it in order to get universal credit or to increase the amount of universal credit you get. This rule will not apply to you if you have used the capital to:

• reduce or pay a debt
• pay for goods or services which are considered reasonable

If you and your partner have capital of over £16,000, you cannot get universal credit. If your capital is over £6,000 but £16,000 or less, you are treated as having an income of £4.35 a month for every £250 (or part of £250) over £6,000.

EXAMPLE

Income from capital

Lauren has £7,400 savings. She is treated as having an income from this capital of £26.10 a month (6 x £4.35). This income reduces her maximum universal credit pound for pound.

---

3. How much universal credit do you get?

How do you calculate universal credit?

Follow the steps below to work out your entitlement. Universal credit is worked out on a month by month basis.

The 'benefit cap' can affect the amount of universal credit you get. There is more information on this on page 42.

Step 1: calculate your maximum universal credit
Add together the 'standard allowance', any additional amounts because you have children, any additional amounts for special circumstances (such as limited capability for work element, carer element or childcare costs element) and any housing costs element. The total is your maximum universal credit.

If you have no other income, this is the amount of universal credit you will get.

If you have other income, go to Step 2.

Step 2: work out your income other than earnings
Your income might include other benefits (such as contributory employment and support allowance), an occupational pension or any income from capital you have between the lower limit and higher limit. Remember that some benefits, including disability living allowance, personal independence payment and child benefit, are ignored. The monthly amount of income is used in the calculation.

If you have no unearned income, go to Step 4.

Step 3: deduct the answer at Step 2 from the answer at Step 1
If you have no earned income, this is the amount of universal credit you will get.

If you have earned income, go to Step 4.

Step 4: work out your earnings
Work out your net earnings for the month after tax, national insurance and any contribution you make to an occupational

pension. If you are an employee, this is usually the amount reported by your employer through 'real-time infomation', so normally it is the same as the information on your payslip. If you are self-employed you may be treated as having higher earnings than you actually have.

Step 5: work out how much of your earnings count

Check which 'work allowance' applies to you and deduct the work allowance from your net earnings (Step 4).

Calculate 65 per cent of this figure.

Step 6: work out how your earnings affect your universal credit

Deduct the answer at Step 5 from Step 1 if you have no unearned income, or from Step 3 if you have unearned income as well as earnings.

This is the amount of universal credit you get.

EXAMPLE

Lone parent with two children

Sophia is aged 30. She lives in a housing association rented property which is the right size for the family. Her rent is £480 a month. She does not have any health problems and she is not looking after a severely disabled person. Her children do not have any disabilities. She has no other income apart from child benefit. Her monthly universal credit is calculated as follows.

Step 1: calculate your maximum universal credit

Standard allowance £311.55

Amount for two children £498.75

Amount for housing costs £480.00

Total = £1,290.30

Sophia has no income apart from child benefit, which is disregarded. She therefore gets the maximum amount of universal credit (£1,290.30). She does not need to follow the remaining steps.

EXAMPLE

Couple with one child

Bob and Gwen are aged 31 and 32. They live in a local authority flat which is the right size for them. Their rent is £250 a month. Their child has a disability and receives the lowest rate care component of disability living allowance. Their only other income is child benefit and contributory employment and support allowance of £433.98 a month, which Bob gets because he has limited capability for work. Their monthly universal credit is calculated as follows.

Step 1: calculate your maximum universal credit
Standard allowance £489.06

Amount for one child £272.08

Amount for disabled child £123.62

Amount for limited capability for work £123.62

Amount for housing costs £250.00

Total = £1,258.38

Step 2: work out your income other than earnings
Employment and support allowance £433.98

Step 3: deduct the answer at Step 2 from the answer at Step 1
£1,258.38 − £433.98 = £824.40

Because they do not have any earned income, this is the amount of universal credit they will get. They do not need to follow the remaining steps.

Note: disability living allowance and child benefit are disregarded, but employment and support allowance is deducted.

EXAMPLE

Single person

Imran is aged 24. He is single and has no children. He has a disability and receives the middle rate care component and higher rate mobility component of disability living allowance. It is accepted that he has limited capability for work. He lives in a housing association flat which is the right size for him. His rent is £400 a month. Imran also has net earnings of £416 a month. His monthly universal credit is calculated as follows.

Step 1: calculate your maximum universal credit
Standard allowance £246.81

Amount for limited capability for work £123.62

Amount for housing costs £400.00

Total = £770.43

Step 2: work out income other than earnings
Disability living allowance is disregarded and therefore Imran has no income apart from his earnings. He can go to Step 4.

Step 4: work out your earnings
Imran has £416.00 a month net earnings.

Step 5: work out how much of your earnings count
The work allowance which applies to Imran is £192.00.

£416.00 – £192.00 = £224.00

£224.00 x 65% = £145.60

Step 6: work out how your earnings affect your universal credit
Deduct the answer at Step 5 from the answer at Step 1 because Imran has no unearned income.

£770.43 – £145.60 = £624.83

This is Imran's universal credit award.

EXAMPLE

Couple with one child

Carl and Meg are a couple aged 30 and 29. They have one child. Meg works and earns £700 net a month. Carl is on contributory employment and support allowance of £433.98 a month because he has limited capability for work. Their only other income is child benefit. They live in a housing association house which is the right size for them. The rent is £450 a month. They have no childcare costs. Their universal credit is calculated as follows.

Step 1: calculate your maximum universal credit
Standard allowance £489.06

Amount for one child £272.08

Amount for limited capability for work £123.62

Amount for housing costs £450.00

Total = £1,334.76

Step 2: work out income other than earnings
Carl's employment and support allowance of £433.98 counts in full as income.

Step 3: deduct the answer at Step 2 from the answer at Step 1
£1,334.76 − £433.98 = £900.78

Step 4: work out your earnings
Meg has £700.00 a month net earnings.

Step 5: work out how much of your earnings count
The work allowance which applies to Meg and Carl is £222.

£700.00 − £222.00 = £478.00

478.00 x 65% = £310.70

Step 6: work out how your earnings affect your universal credit
Deduct the answer at Step 5 from the answer at Step 3 as they
have unearned income as well as earnings.

£900.78 – £310.70 = £590.08

This is Carl and Meg's universal credit award.

Are you being transferred to universal credit?

If you are getting one of the benefits being abolished because of the
introduction of universal credit, you will stay on that benefit until the
DWP decides it is time to transfer your claim to universal credit. This
transfer process is due to end by 2017.

If you then become entitled to universal credit, 'transitional
protection' will ensure that the amount you get when you move
onto universal credit will be the same as you were getting on your
previous benefit. This should ensure that the amount of universal
credit you get at the point of transfer will not be less than the
amount you were previously getting. You will stay on the same level
of benefit without any increases (if your circumstances do not
change), until the universal credit amounts catch up over time. You
will only get this transitional protection if your claim is transferred for
you, not if you are allowed to claim universal credit because of a
change in circumstances. Your transitional protection will end
completely if there is a significant change in your circumstances – eg,
if a partner leaves or joins your household.

The benefit cap

What the law says

The benefit cap

The 'benefit cap' means that your benefit entitlement is capped at the level of average household earnings (£1,517 a month if you are single with no dependent children, and £2,167 a month otherwise). Benefit entitlement includes universal credit and most other benefits, but does not include pension credit or retirement pension. If your benefit entitlement is more than the cap level, the excess is deducted from your universal credit. If you have an amount for the childcare costs element included in your universal credit, this amount is deducted from the excess before your universal credit is reduced. If the childcare costs element is more than the excess, no deduction is made.

Regulations 78 to 83 The Universal Credit Regulations 2013

Are you exempt from the benefit cap?

Some people are exempt from the benefit cap. These include if you:

- are getting disability living allowance (or your child gets disability living allowance), personal independence payment, attendance allowance or industrial injuries disablement benefit
- have both limited capability for work and work-related activity
- are a war pensioner, or a war widow or war widower
- earn £430 or more a month

If you have been working for a year or more earning £430 or more a month and you stop working, you are exempt from the benefit cap for nine months.

What CPAG says

The benefit cap

According to the government, the benefit cap is based on fairness because it will prevent households on benefits having a higher income than those in work. The comparison is not, however, made on a like-for-like basis, as it does not take into account the full income of in-work households in comparable situations. This is because only wages are counted and other not in-work benefits.

The government estimates that around 50,000 households will lose an average of £93 a week as a result of the cap. More than 90 per cent of those affected are likely to be families with children; 80 per cent will have three or more children; 40 per cent will have five or more children.

Also, the benefit cap may make it difficult for families to become kinship carers or for couples to stay together in larger merged households.

CPAG believes that the cap is unfair and damaging to children, and should be removed. At the very least, benefits for children, such as child benefit and amounts for children in universal credit, should be removed from the cap.

Further information

There is more information about universal credit amounts and how income and capital is worked out in CPAG's *Welfare Benefits and Tax Credits Handbook*.

Chapter 4
Claiming universal credit

This chapter covers:

1. Who should claim universal credit?

2. How do you make a claim?

3. When should you claim?

4. How are you paid?

5. Reporting changes in your circumstances

What you need to know

- You make a joint claim for universal credit if you are in a couple. If you are a lone parent or a single person, you make a single claim.
- The usual way to claim is online, although some people can claim by telephone or in person.
- Universal credit is normally paid directly into your bank account. Couples can have a joint account or choose which one will receive the payment.
- Payments are normally made monthly. Payment for rent is paid to you, not direct to your landlord. There are 'alternative payment arrangements' for some people who need help managing their money.
- You can check your award and payments using your online account. You do not need to report changes in your earnings if your employer is using the 'real-time information' system to report your earnings every time you are paid. You do need to report any other changes yourself.

1. Who should claim universal credit?

Universal credit is a benefit to provide support for adults and children. If you are single or a lone parent, you claim for yourself as a single person. If you are in a couple, you make a joint claim.

What the law says

Are you in a couple?

Usually it is clear whether or not you are in a couple, but there are rules about this.

- You and your partner are a couple if you are married and living in the same household.

- You and your partner are a couple if you are not married but 'living together as husband and wife'.

- You and your partner are a couple if you are the same sex, and are registered as civil partners and living in the same household.

- You and your partner are a couple if you are the same sex and not civil partners, but 'living together as though you were civil partners'.

Sections 2 and 39 Welfare Reform Act 2012

The Department for Work and Pensions (DWP) decides whether you are 'living together as husband and wife' or 'as though you were civil partners' by looking at various factors like whether you have the same address, the type of relationship you have, whether you have children and your financial arrangements.

Although the usual rule is that you claim universal credit jointly as a couple, sometimes only one of you is allowed to claim. In that case, you claim as a single person. See Box A.

Box A

When do you claim as a single person even though you are in a couple?

- One of you is under 18 (which is the usual age limit for claiming universal credit). However, you make a joint claim if you have a child or if you are allowed to claim at age 16 or 17 for another reason. These are explained in Chapter 2. Couples where both are under 18 may make a single or joint claim depending on whether one or both are allowed to claim at that age.

- Your partner does not meet the immigration or residence conditions for universal credit – eg, s/he is abroad when you claim, or does not have a 'right to reside' or is a 'person subject to immigration control'.

- Your partner was in Great Britain when you made your claim but since then has been abroad for longer than a month, or sometimes more.

- Your partner is in prison.

- Your partner is temporarily away from home and has been away for more than six months or you expect to be apart for longer than this. In this case, you do not get any amount for your partner in your award, and only your own income and capital is taken into account.

Make sure you give details about both of you when you claim, because while you do not get any amount for your partner in your award, joint income and capital are still taken into account and your partner's circumstances still count if you are claiming a childcare costs element.

What if you start or end a relationship?

If you were claiming jointly as a couple but have separated from your partner, tell the DWP. You can then make a fresh claim for universal credit based on your new circumstances. You should claim as soon as possible but, as long as you do so within a month of the award stopping, you can ask for your new claim to be backdated. If your former partner has already told the DWP, your own award can be reassessed without you making a fresh claim.

If you become a couple (eg, you and your partner start living together), as long as at least one of you was getting universal credit already, you do not need to make a fresh claim. You do have to tell the DWP about the change in your situation and give any information required.

If you cannot claim for yourself

If you cannot claim for yourself, perhaps because you have a mental health problem or learning disability, someone else (called an 'appointee'), who might be a friend or relative, can be authorised to claim on your behalf. If you have a partner, s/he could make the joint claim for both of you.

2. How do you make a claim?

You claim universal credit:

* online at www.gov.uk/universal-credit
* by telephone if you cannot claim online
* in person if you really need to claim this way

The usual way to claim universal credit is online. The website first checks whether you are eligible to claim in your area. If you are eligible, the online instructions take you through the claim. There is a telephone helpline you can call if you need help while you are going through the online claim (0845 600 0723; textphone 0845 600 0743).

Box B

What happens when you claim universal credit?

- When you are ready to claim, have your national insurance number to hand and details of any income that is not from work, any other benefits you or your partner get, any savings or capital, rent agreement and bank account details.

- Completing the claim is likely to take up to 40 minutes.

- When you get to the end of your online claim, you are given a summary of the information you have entered. You have a chance to go back and correct any mistakes. When you are happy the information is correct, you submit your claim.

- You will then be shown the amount of universal credit you are likely to get based on the information in your claim.

- After you submit your claim, the DWP may call you to tell you when to come for an interview at the jobcentre and tell you what documents you need to bring with you. Not everybody is expected to attend interviews.

- If you do have to go to an interview, you will see an adviser who will confirm your identity and ask you to sign a copy of your claim details. The adviser will also discuss what work you will be expected to prepare for or look for, and will ask you to sign a 'claimant commitment' which is a record of what you are expected to do. You must sign this or your claim will stop.

- You are sent a decision letter telling you how much universal credit you are entitled to.

If you cannot make your claim online

Not everyone has online access at home or is able to use the internet. Your local jobcentre may help or can direct you to local organisations who can help you make your claim. Your local authority may provide computers with internet access that you can use – eg, in local libraries.

If you cannot claim online, you can claim by telephone. An adviser will take your details and complete an online claim for you. If you cannot use the telephone, you can ask to claim in person, for example, at a local office or by an adviser visiting you at home. However, this is intended to be exceptional. If you do claim by telephone or in person, your claim starts when you first contact the DWP to say you want to claim, so it is important to do so quickly if you cannot claim online.

There is no paper claim form for universal credit.

3. When should you claim?

Universal credit is being introduced gradually across the country between October 2013 and April 2014. You can only claim when it is introduced in your area and the DWP begins inviting claims. If you are already getting benefit, you may be transferred to universal credit at a later date. There is more information about transferring to universal credit in Chapter 8.

There are general rules about making claims that affect when entitlement can begin. Usually your entitlement starts when you submit your claim, so it is important not to delay. However, it is sometimes possible for a claim to be backdated.

When can your claim be backdated?

If any of the following reasons apply to you and meant you could not reasonably claim earlier, ask the DWP to backdate your claim for up to a month:

- you have a disability
- you send a medical certificate to say that you could not claim earlier because you were ill

- you were getting jobseeker's allowance or employment and support allowance which ended, but you were only notified after it ended
- you could not claim online because the system was not working
- you were in a couple but are now claiming as a single person and your former partner did not accept a 'claimant commitment' which meant that your joint claim was refused or stopped

Remember, if you are a couple claiming jointly, both of you must be in one of these circumstances.

EXAMPLES

When to claim

Amina is aged 20 and has just had her first baby. She is a lone parent. A week after the baby is born, she completes the online claim for universal credit. Her award is not backdated and she misses out on a week's money.

Darius has been in hospital after having a heart attack. He is self-employed and has not been able to work for three weeks. When he gets home he claims universal credit. He asks for it to be backdated and sends in his medical certificate. The DWP accepts that he could not reasonably claim earlier and backdates his award.

Joe lost his job on Monday. He needs help to make an online claim for universal credit. As he has no computer himself and is not confident about using one, on Saturday he goes to his daughter's house and with her help submits his online claim. His award is not backdated. (If Joe had telephoned the DWP to ask to claim by telephone, his award could have started from the date he called.)

Getting your decision

Initially the DWP plans to send universal credit decision letters by post. Eventually, more communication will be online.

The responsibility for making a decision on your claim lies with a decision maker in the DWP. In most cases, the assessment of your claim and the calculation of your award will be done automatically by computer.

4. How are you paid?

Universal credit is paid directly into your bank or building society account in monthly payments. It is paid in arrears. From the date you claim you will need to wait for one month and up to another seven days to get your first payment. You are then paid on the same day each month after that. If this falls at a weekend or bank holiday, you are paid on the nearest working day before that. The amount you get does not change depending on the number of days in the month.

If you are in a couple and claiming jointly, universal credit is normally paid in one amount. It is up to you to decide whose account it is paid into or you can have a joint account. If you cannot decide, the DWP can make the decision. Exceptionally, the payment could be split between you, or paid to the other partner if the DWP decides that is in your or your child's interest.

Are you having trouble making the money last?

When you claim universal credit, you are offered advice about budgeting which may be online, by telephone or face to face at a local money advice service. If you need more help, you can ask for 'alternative payment arrangements' or the DWP may decide to make these arrangements without your asking. There are three main alternative payment arrangements:

- you can be paid twice a month
- your rent can be paid directly to your landlord
- your payment can be split between you and your partner

The DWP decides whether you can be paid this way, and you cannot appeal if you disagree. The decision is based on guidance and depends on your circumstances. See Box C.

Box C

Alternative payment arrangements

You are most likely to be accepted for an alternative payment arrangement if you:

- have rent arrears or are threatened with eviction or repossession
- have severe debt problems
- have difficulty reading or writing, or with simple mathematics
- have a learning disability or a mental health condition
- have an alcohol, drug or gambling addiction
- are under 18 or a care leaver
- are homeless or in temporary or supported accommodation
- are, or were, experiencing domestic abuse
- are a family with multiple or complex needs

There are other reasons given in guidance why someone might have difficulty managing so it is worth explaining why you need this help.

EXAMPLE

Alternative payment arrangements

Gemma is a lone parent of two children. To find the money to keep up with loan repayments, she has missed rent payments and is now nearly two months in arrears. She suffers from anxiety and depression and one of her children is not coping well at school. Gemma explains her circumstances to the DWP and asks for her rent to be paid directly to her landlord. This is agreed and Gemma is also signposted to a local money advice service for debt and budgeting advice.

What can you do if there is a delay in getting paid?

You might need some money to tide you over while you wait for your first universal credit payment or while you wait for your award to increase after a change of circumstances such as leaving a job. In these circumstances, you can ask for an advance payment of universal credit. This is known as a 'short-term advance'. If there is a delay on only one part of your claim (eg, if there is still some information or evidence needed to decide how much housing costs to pay), you can ask for the remainder of your universal credit award to be paid in the meantime as a short-term advance. You pay back the advance out of your universal credit award.

The DWP will only give you a short-term advance if it thinks there is a serious risk of damage to the health or safety of you or your family. You cannot appeal if it is refused, but you can provide more information about your situation and ask the DWP to reconsider.

EXAMPLE

Short-term advance

Carmine is a lone parent with one child. She works part time and rents her home. Carmine claims universal credit. She has been asked to provide proof of the rent she pays, but she does not have a rent book and is having trouble getting the evidence she needs from her landlord. Carmine's part-time wages are not enough to feed the family and pay the bills. She asks for a short-term advance. The DWP decides in the meantime to pay Carmen all her universal credit, except for her housing costs, as a short-term advance, and tells her it will be deducted from the arrears of the amount she is due once the award is decided.

What can you do if you need a loan?

If you need a loan for a household item you cannot afford or to meet expenses for a new baby or a new job for example, you can ask for an advance of universal credit called a 'budgeting advance'. You can ask for a budgeting advance for whatever you need, but if you are refused you cannot appeal. To qualify you must have been on universal credit for at least six months (or income support, income-based jobseeker's allowance, income-related employment and support allowance or pension credit) unless you need the advance to help you get work or stay in work. Your earnings and any savings or capital resources must be below a certain level. The maximum you can get depends on your family size (if you have a child, you can get up to £812).

You pay back the advance out of your universal credit award each month. You need to pay it back in full before you can ask for another budgeting advance.

EXAMPLE

Budgeting advance

Emma is a lone parent and is getting universal credit. Her washing machine has broken down and she needs a new one. Instead of buying one with expensive high street credit, she asks for a budgeting advance of her universal credit. She pays this back out of her monthly award.

Paying universal credit to other people

The DWP can pay part of your universal credit directly to a third party on your behalf. For example, if you have a mortgage, the amount in your universal credit for mortgage interest may be paid directly to your lender.

If you rent your home, normally the amount for rent in your universal credit is paid to you as part of your monthly award, and not to your landlord. It is paid this way whether you rent from a local authority, housing association or private landlord. However, if you are finding it difficult to budget or are building up rent arrears, the DWP may decide to pay your landlord directly under the 'alternative payment arrangements' – see Box C. You can also have amounts deducted from your universal credit to repay arrears of fuel bills and other essential services.

5. Reporting changes in your circumstances

You normally have an online account for your universal credit award. This allows you to check the information about your claim and payments. In time, you will be able to report changes in your circumstances online. If you cannot use the internet, there are other ways to report changes in your circumstances – eg, by telephone or face to face with an adviser. To begin with, when universal credit is introduced, instead of using your online account, you may be asked to use the telephone helpline to report changes. When you report a change, you should get a letter to confirm the change and tell you how your award is affected.

If you are employed, you do not normally need to report changes in your earnings. The DWP will get information on your earnings from HM Revenue and Customs (HMRC) through its new 'real-time information system'. Under this system, your employer sends HMRC information about your earnings every time you are paid. If your employer is not using this system yet, you will need to report your take-home pay yourself every month.

EXAMPLE

Reporting self-employed earnings

Matt is self-employed. He gets a message from the DWP reminding him to report his self-employed earnings for the month 12 February to 12 March (his 'assessment period'). Matt is busy and does not get round to it. His universal credit award is not paid when it is next due and the DWP tells him it has been suspended. He needs to send in the missing earnings report quickly, otherwise his award will stop altogether.

If you are self-employed, you are expected to report your earnings every month on a 'cash in/cash out' basis – ie, income received during the month and payments you have made for the business that month if they come under set categories. The DWP plans to send self-employed people a message each month to remind them of the reporting deadline. If you miss the deadline, your award is suspended.

If you pay for childcare, you must report your childcare charges each month.

How do changes affect your award?

You are paid a month in arrears, so every payment you get is based on circumstances in the previous month. When you report a change in your circumstances, you must wait until your next usual universal credit payday before your award goes up or down. The revised amount is normally worked out as though your new circumstances had lasted for the whole of the previous month. Here a 'month' means the monthly 'assessment period' on which your payment is based. You are paid a few days after the end of the assessment period and are expected to report any changes before the end of that period.

If you are late reporting a change (being late means that you report it after the end of the assessment period in which the change took place), and your award goes up because of the change, you will not get arrears paid before the month you actually reported it, so you will lose money. There is a rule that allows the DWP to backdate an increased award if there are special circumstances. So it is always worth saying why you are reporting a change late and explaining any difficulties you had, such as ill health.

If your award goes down because of the change, this is backdated, so if you are late reporting the change you will have an overpayment. The later you report the change, the more you will need to pay back – and it is possible you might be asked to pay a fine as well (there is more about fines in Chapter 6).

EXAMPLES

How changes affect awards

Poonam has a new baby born one week after the start of a new assessment period (the month on which the next payment of universal credit is based). She tells the DWP about the baby before the end of the same assessment period. Her next payment includes an amount for the new baby for the whole of the month in which the baby was born, even though the baby was born a week into the month.

Danni has a new baby born two weeks after the start of a new assessment period. She is depressed and tired after the birth and does not call the DWP until four weeks after the birth. This is halfway through the next assessment period. Her next payment includes an amount for the baby for the whole of the assessment period after the one in which the baby was born. She has lost a month's extra money. If Danni had explained why she was late reporting the birth, the DWP could have decided to pay her the first month's money.

Steve starts university and is no longer entitled to universal credit in his circumstances. His course starts one week before the end of his assessment period. He tells the DWP as soon as his course starts. His award stops and he does not get any universal credit for the whole of the assessment period in which he started his course.

What CPAG says

Claims and payments

CPAG is concerned about the potential effects of a number of the universal credit provisions, including the move to online claiming, monthly payments, that payments are made to just one person in the household, and that a single payment could be 'all or nothing'.

With the expectation that people normally make and manage their claims online, CPAG is concerned that those without a computer at home, or who cannot use the internet, could face difficulties if other ways to claim and to access messages and decisions are not made widely available.

With universal credit payments being monthly instead of fortnightly as they are for most other benefits, there is concern that many people on low incomes will find it hard to budget. When this happens, mothers in particular tend to go without.

With support for adults and children included in one payment, CPAG believes that money meant for children should go to the main carer, usually the mother.

In the benefits system, it is common for a claim to be delayed or for payments to be suspended while the DWP clarifies evidence or waits to make a decision. Under universal credit, all support depends on one payment, and so the consequences of delay or suspension could be that someone is left with no means of support.

As well as monthly payments, universal credit relies on monthly reassessments of earnings. If employers fail to report earnings under the 'real-time information' system, CPAG is concerned that claimants will lose out. For the self-employed, having to report earnings each month is a time-consuming burden where any delay could leave families short of money, and which could act as a barrier to entering self-employment.

Further information

There is draft guidance on universal credit alternative payment arrangements at www.gov.uk/government/publications/universal-credit-local-support-services-framework.

If you are working with people claiming universal credit, there is a government universal credit toolkit for advisers at www.gov.uk/government/publications/specialist-guides/advice-for-decision-making/.

There is more information about universal credit claims and payments in CPAG's *Welfare Benefits and Tax Credits Handbook*.

Chapter 5
Your claimant commitment

This chapter covers:

1. What is the claimant commitment?

2. What are you expected to do?

3. Who has no work-related requirements?

4. Who must take part in work-focused interviews?

5. Who must prepare for work?

6. Who must look for work?

What you need to know

- When you claim universal credit, you (and your partner if you have one) must accept a 'claimant commitment'.

- Your claimant commitment lists your 'work-related requirements' while getting universal credit. These vary from not having to do anything, to being available for and looking for full-time work.

- The government accepts that some groups will need to claim universal credit in the longer term and not be able to move into work. If you are in one of these groups, you may have no work-related requirements at all.

- You (and your partner if you have one) must meet a set of personalised requirements.

- If you already work, you may be expected to look for more work or better paid work, if your earnings are low.

1. What is the claimant commitment?

If you claim universal credit, you normally have to accept a 'claimant commitment' before you can get any benefit. If you have a partner, you each have to accept a commitment individually. The content of your claimant commitment is set by the Department for Work and Pensions (DWP), which also decides whether it should be changed.

What does a claimant commitment include?

The 'claimant commitment' is a kind of contract between you and the DWP. It sets out what you must do in return for receiving universal credit. One of the most important areas of the claimant commitment is the 'work-related requirements' that are expected of you. The information that is likely to be included in the claimant commitment is explained in Box A.

Box A
What is likely to be included in the claimant commitment?

- What your work-related requirements are. What this means is explained in the rest of this chapter.

- Depending on what your requirements are, it can include details of what specific things you must do, and by when.

- How much your universal credit will be reduced by, and how long for, if you do not meet your requirements.

- What kind of changes or circumstances you must report, and what happens if you do not do this.

- That you have the right to challenge a decision to reduce your universal credit because you have not met your requirements.

There is more information about reductions to universal credit awards – called sanctions – in Chapter 6. Chapter 7 contains information about how to challenge a decision if you disagree with it.

If you must look for work, your claimant commitment also includes the number of hours you are expected to be available for work. This is normally 35 hours a week, but may be fewer hours if you are allowed to restrict your availability for work – eg, if you are the 'responsible carer' of a child under 13.

If you are claiming jobseeker's allowance or employment and support allowance at the same time as universal credit, you only have work-related requirements for universal credit, not for the other benefit you get.

EXAMPLE

The claimant commitment

Jenny is 32 and lives alone. She loses her job and claims universal credit. Her claimant commitment says that she is looking for work and will do anything she can to get work. It states that she must be available for full-time work and what hours she is able to work. There is a section about the type of work that she is looking for initially, and what she must do every week to look for work. This includes regular things she must do every week, and specific actions to be taken by the end of the month. It explains that she must go to appointments with her personal adviser when asked. It lists changes of circumstances that she must report, and the consequences if she does not report changes. It tells her about the sanctions that may apply if she does not meet her work-related requirements. It explains her right of appeal if her universal credit is sanctioned.

How do you accept a claimant commitment?

If you have few or no work-related requirements, you can normally accept your commitment as part of the online claims process. If you must prepare for or look for work, the contents of your commitment are normally agreed at an initial interview with an adviser, as what it says will depend on your skills, qualifications and work history. You will be told when you need to accept your claimant commitment by.

What the law says

Accepting your claimant commitment

The DWP decides how you must accept your claimant commitment. You can be asked to accept it either:

- online
- by telephone
- in person

If you do not accept your claimant commitment within the time allowed by the DWP after you claim, you normally do not get any universal credit until the day you finally accept it.

Reg 15 Universal Credit Regulations 2013

The circumstances in which the different kinds of work-related requirements apply are explained in the rest of this chapter.

What happens if you do not accept a claimant commitment?

If you do not accept a claimant commitment, you are not entitled to universal credit at all. If you are part of a couple, you must both accept a commitment to be entitled.

You do not have to accept a claimant commitment if you lack the capacity to do so. This is most likely if you have an 'appointee' who is responsible for your universal credit claim. You may also be entitled without agreeing a commitment in exceptional circumstances such as the jobcentre being closed unexpectedly, an emergency at home or if you are in hospital. You must accept a commitment as soon as you can do so, and should explain to the DWP why you were not able to accept your commitment earlier.

If you do not agree with the work-related requirements set out in your claimant commitment, then you may be offered a 'cooling-off period' to think about this before a decision is made that you are not entitled to universal credit. If you are unhappy with the things you must do, you can ask for this to be reviewed. However, unless the

DWP decides that your request is reasonable, you are not entitled to any universal credit until the day you accept the commitment.

Can you change your claimant commitment?

The rest of this chapter explains when you must be given a particular kind of work-related requirement, and when this will be at the discretion of an adviser. Changes may be made by discussion and negotiation with you, but the law normally gives the DWP the power to decide when and how your commitment is updated. Your commitment will be updated regularly if you must look for work, as you agree specific actions with your personal adviser. You must agree to the updated version to still be entitled to universal credit.

Your commitment must be changed if there is a relevant change in your circumstances – eg, you adopt a child or become entitled to a carer element in your award. If you are unhappy with what your claimant commitment says you must do, you can ask for this to be reviewed by the DWP. However, you may be sanctioned unless you continue to meet your work-related requirements while the commitment is being reviewed.

2. What are you expected to do?

The remaining sections of this chapter explain the different kinds of work-related requirements and when they apply to you. There are four broad groups, each with different levels of work-related requirements. Use the table to identify the group you are likely to be in. Remember that your partner may be in a different group to you. If you are an European Economic Area national, you and your partner may have all of the work-related requirements even if your circumstances mean you would normally have fewer requirements. See Chapter 9 for more information.

Which work-related requirements do you have?

Group	Work-related requirements
You are caring for a severely disabled person	No work-related requirements
You have 'limited capability for work-related activity'	
You are heavily pregnant or have recently given birth	
You are the lone parent or responsible carer of a child under one	
You are the responsible carer of a child you have adopted within the past year	
You earn above a certain amount (your 'earnings threshold')	
You are over the age at which you could claim pension credit	
You are a student getting a loan or certain grants	
You are a young person in non-advanced education who is 'without parental support'	
You have recently experienced domestic violence	
You are a lone parent or the responsible carer of a child aged under five	Work-focused interviews only
You are a single foster carer of a child under 16, or the responsible foster carer in a couple	
You have started caring for the child of a family member or friend within the past year	
You have 'limited capability for work'	Work preparation and work-focused interviews
You are a jobseeker, or you are not in one of the above groups	All work-related requirements
You are doing some work, but are not in one of the above groups	

Who helps you move towards work?

The government introduced a new initiative, called the Work Programme, in summer 2011. This is delivered by at least two main organisations in each region of the UK, who may then sub contract other organisations to help you get work. You can be referred to this programme if you must look for or prepare for work. If you are looking for work, you may still have to 'sign on' at the Jobcentre Plus office, or you may instead review your work search with a DWP adviser over the phone or online. You may be referred to the Work Programme for further help.

There are other schemes which are not delivered directly by the DWP, which you may also be referred to as part of your work-related requirements. These include unpaid work placements and short-term projects focused on promoting employment in a particular sector. What you must do should be set out in your claimant commitment.

Most people will not be immediately referred to the Work Programme. When you claim universal credit, an adviser in your local Jobcentre Plus office will be responsible for helping you to meet your 'work-related requirements'.

In the longer term, the main person helping you to look for or prepare for work (your 'personal adviser') may not be employed by the DWP. Although this could be the person you see most often, the actual decisions about your universal credit entitlement, including whether it should be 'sanctioned', are still made by a decision maker in the DWP. Your personal adviser may make recommendations to the decision maker.

3. Who has no work-related requirements?

In certain circumstances, you cannot be asked to undertake any work-related requirements to get universal credit. Even if one of the circumstances in this section applies to you, you must still agree a claimant commitment to be entitled to universal credit.

Are you caring for a severely disabled person?

You have no work-related requirements if you get a carer element in your universal credit. You get this element if you care for a severely disabled person for at least 35 hours a week, and no one else gets it for caring for the same person. You do not count as a carer under these rules if you are working as a paid carer, or if you are in full-time education.

The definition of who is a 'severely disabled person' is linked to the rate of disability living allowance, personal independence payment or attendance allowance received by the person you care for. All disability living allowance claimants between the ages of 16 and 64 will be reassessed for personal independence payment starting from autumn 2013. This may affect your work-related requirements if the person you care for does not qualify for personal independence payment for help with daily living needs, as this will mean that s/he no longer counts as a severely disabled person.

If you do not qualify for the carer element – perhaps because someone else gets it for looking after the same severely disabled person – but you spend 35 hours or more a week caring, then you may still not have any work-related requirements. However, this decision will be at the discretion of the DWP, who must accept that it would be unreasonable for you to look for any work at all.

There is more information about universal credit and carers in Chapter 9.

Are you over pension age?

If you are over the age at which you would not be able to claim universal credit as a single person, but you must claim universal credit because you live with a younger partner, then you have no work-related requirements. Your partner may still have some work-related requirements. There is more information about the age limits for claiming universal credit in Chapter 2, and more information about older people and universal credit in Chapter 9.

Are you pregnant or caring for a child under one?

If you are pregnant and it is less than 11 weeks until the week in which your baby is due, you have no work-related requirements. You also have no requirements for 15 weeks after giving birth. If you have a child under one included as part of your family in your universal credit award or you are fostering a child under one, and you are either a lone parent or the 'responsible carer' in a couple, you have no work-related requirements. You and your partner can decide jointly who is the responsible carer of a child, but only one of you can be the responsible carer, even if you have more than one child.

You are able to change who the responsible carer is once a year (starting from the date of the previous nomination), or if the decision maker accepts that there has been a relevant change in your household circumstances.

EXAMPLE

The responsible carer

Luis and Patricia have a joint claim for universal credit. When their son Pablo is born, they nominate Patricia as the responsible carer. She has no work-related requirements, and Luis is looking for work. Patricia is offered a job when Pablo is six months old. She cannot take the job unless there is someone else to look after Pablo, so the couple decide to nominate Luis as the responsible carer instead. The decision maker agrees and Luis no longer has to look for work. Patricia is able to take the job while Luis looks after Pablo.

Have you recently adopted a child?

If you are the responsible carer of a child that you have been matched with for adoption, you have no work-related requirements for a one-year period after the child is placed with you. If you want, you can choose that this period starts up to two weeks before the child is actually placed with you. These rules do not apply if, before adopting, you were a foster parent or relative of the child.

Do you have 'limited capability for work-related activity'?

The severity of your health problem or disability is decided by using a test designed to identify whether your illness or disability is so serious that you should not be expected to prepare for a return to work at the moment.

There is more information about this test in Chapter 3.

Are you a student?

If you are a full-time student and you receive a grant or loan that is counted as income for universal credit, you have no work-related requirements. Remember that most students are not eligible to claim universal credit at all. This is explained in Chapter 2. This rule applies to you during the months in which your student income is taken into account in calculating your universal credit award, so you may still have some work-related requirements during the long summer vacation.

You also do not have any work-related requirements if you are a young student who is able to claim universal credit as you do not get any support from your parents.

Have you recently experienced domestic violence?

Even if you would normally have to meet some or all of the work-related requirements, you do not have to do so for 13 weeks if you have experienced domestic violence. You must tell the DWP within six months of the violence, no longer live with the perpetrator and, within one month of your notification, you must provide evidence from a professional that the abuse is likely to have occurred. You can only be exempted from your work-related requirements due to domestic violence once in any one-year period.

The definition of 'domestic violence' includes controlling or coercive behaviour or actual or threatened physical, financial, psychological, emotional or sexual abuse, and the perpetrator was either your partner or certain other relatives.

Do you earn above a certain amount?

Once you (and your partner if you have one) have more than a certain amount of earnings, you are not expected to look for more work. This is called the 'earnings threshold'. If you would otherwise have to look for work, your individual earnings threshold is set at the amount you would earn if you worked the number of hours that your claimant commitment says you must be available for work for, and you were paid at the national minimum wage. If you are not in the group who must look for work, then you have no work-related requirements if you earn over 16 times the national minimum wage a week. The threshold is based on your average weekly earnings, before deducting any tax and national insurance contributions that you must pay.

If you are an apprentice, you have no work-related requirements if your weekly earnings are over 30 times the hourly minimum wage for an apprentice your age, unless you have been allowed to restrict your availability for work to below 30 hours a week.

The earnings threshold also applies if you are self-employed and your earnings are low, and you have started your business within the last year. If you have been self-employed for over a year and it is your main employment, you are treated as earning the amount of your individual threshold even if you actually earn less than this, unless you are not expected to look for work due to your other circumstances.

There is more information about how your earnings are calculated if you are self-employed in Chapter 3.

If you live with your partner, you also have a joint earnings threshold. This is the total amount you would earn if you both earned the amount that is your individual threshold. If your joint income is above the threshold, it does not matter how much you each earn individually. If your joint income is below the threshold, normally you are both expected to look for work. However, if you already earn more than your individual threshold, but your partner does not, you do not have to look for more work, but your partner does.

If you live with a partner but must claim universal credit as a single person, your joint earnings threshold is calculated as if your partner was expected to work 35 hours a week.

If your earnings vary from week to week, you are above your earnings threshold if your average weekly earnings are more than the threshold. If you have a normal cycle of work, your earnings are averaged over one cycle. If not, your earnings are normally averaged over three months.

A lower earnings threshold may be accepted in some cases.

EXAMPLE

The earnings threshold

Bob and Derek claim universal credit as a couple in November 2013. They have no children or health problems, and no savings or other income. They are both over 20, so the minimum wage they would get is £6.31 an hour. Their joint earnings threshold is 35 hours multiplied by £6.31, multiplied by two (as they are both expected to look for full-time work). This is £441.70 a week.

A month later, Derek finds a job. He works 40 hours a week and receives £400 a week before tax and national insurance. Derek now has no work-related requirements due to the amount of his earnings, but the couple are still below their joint earnings threshold, so Bob must still be available for and looking for full-time work. However, if he finds a job paying £42 a week or more, the couple's earnings will be above their joint threshold and they will then both have no work-related requirements.

4. Who must take part in work-focused interviews?

If it is accepted that you are unlikely to move into work soon, you may only have to take part in 'work-focused interviews' and have no other work-related requirements as a condition of getting universal credit. You are most likely to be in this group if you look after young children or if you are a foster carer.

What happens at a work-focused interview?

The purpose of a work-focused interview is to discuss how you can remain in or obtain work, including getting more work if you work already. Specific topics are likely to include those listed in Box B.

> Box B
> **What is discussed at a work-focused interview?**
>
> Subjects likely to be discussed at a work-focused interview include:
>
> - any work that you currently do, including self-employment
> - how you can stay in work or increase your earnings
> - your qualifications and training
> - any medical condition or disability you have which may be a barrier to working
> - your caring or childcare responsibilities and how they affect your ability to move into work
> - potential work and training opportunities for the future
> - accessing help and support to assist you to move into work

Are you a foster carer?

There are special rules for registered foster carers who have a child placed with them. If you are looking after the child of a friend or family member who is 'looked after by the local authority', you may count as a foster carer under these rules. If you are a single foster carer or the responsible carer in a couple, you will only have to take part in work-focused interviews until your youngest foster child is 16.

Your partner will normally have the work-related requirements that are appropriate for her/him.

If your foster child has extra care needs, you may not have to look for work after s/he turns 16, if that is accepted as reasonable.

If both you and your partner need to care for your foster child because of the level of her/his extra needs, it is possible that neither of you will have to look for work.

If you are between fostering placements, you do not have any additional work-related requirements for the first eight weeks after your last placement ended, provided you intend to continue fostering.

Are you looking after the child of a friend or family member?

If you are the responsible carer for a child whose parents are not currently able to look after her/him, you may only have to take part in work-focused interviews for the first year after you start looking after the child.

If the child you are looking after is in the care of the local authority, you may instead count as a foster carer and only have to take part in work-focused interviews until the child turns 16.

Are you caring for a child under five?

If you are the lone parent or responsible carer of a child who is at least one year old but not yet five, you must take part in work-focused interviews.

The government has stated that from 2014 onwards, lone parents and responsible carers of a child aged three or four will also have to prepare for work.

EXAMPLE

Work-focused interviews

Anwar is the responsible carer for his daughter Aisha. She is four years old and goes to nursery for three hours every weekday morning. Anwar has to drop her off and pick her up, but he is able to work two hours a day during the time Aisha is at nursery. He has spoken to his manager and is confident that he can increase his hours once Aisha starts school. He must still take part in work-focused interviews when asked to do so.

If Anwar's employer thought he needed to do more training to be ready to increase his working hours, Anwar could discuss this with his personal adviser at an interview to see if there was any help available to do this. This would be on a voluntary basis, as the law only allows for a requirement to take part in work-focused interviews to be imposed on Anwar.

5. Who must prepare for work?

Some people must prepare for work by taking some of the action discussed in their work-focused interviews, but are not expected to look for or take a job. This applies to you if you have 'limited capability for work' but might be expected to move towards work in the future.

Box C
What does preparing for work mean?

Work preparation can include spending a set amount of time on activities including:

- having a skills assessment
- improving your personal presentation
- doing training
- participating in the Work Programme
- doing work experience or work placements

- developing your own business plan
- undertaking a work-focused health-related assessment if you have health problems or a disability

Other activities may be added to the list if your adviser thinks it necessary. You must also attend work-focused interviews if asked to do so.

What does 'limited capability for work' mean?

'Limited capability for a work' is a test of whether your health or disability is a serious barrier to work. As well as affecting your work-related requirements, the test is used to decide whether you qualify for employment and support allowance, and whether you qualify for an additional element of universal credit.

There is more information about this test in Chapter 3.

If it is decided that you do not have limited capability for work and you have appealed against the decision because you disagree with it, you must look for work until your appeal is decided. You may be able to restrict your availability for work using the rules explained in the next section of this chapter.

What do you *not* have to do?

If you must prepare for work, you do not have to look for, apply for or take a job as these are different work-related requirements. However, you could be expected to do work experience or take a placement with an employer. There is no other detail in the law about what you can be asked to do as work preparation. This means that if you have young children at school, you may need to explain this to your personal adviser and ask to only be given work preparation activities that are compatible with school hours.

EXAMPLE

Preparing for work

Thomas has been claiming universal credit for six months. He has bipolar disorder which affects his ability to work. He is assessed as having limited capability for work; so must prepare for work. Thomas used to work in an office, but is worried that his knowledge of computing will not be good enough to get a similar job when he is able to return to work.

He attends a work-focused interview and agrees with his personal adviser that he will attend a two-month computing course to update his skills. His adviser agrees to look for a one week work placement after the course ends, so he can see how well he copes with being at work. A separate assessment of how his mental health will affect his ability to manage a job may be arranged by the adviser.

6. Who must look for work?

If you are not in one of the groups explained in the last three sections (the groups are also listed in the table on page 65), you must look for work. This involves both being 'available for work' and 'actively looking for work'. You must also attend a work-focused interview or prepare for work as well if you are asked to do this.

What does 'being available for work' mean?

The standard definition of 'being available for work' is that you are willing and able to immediately take up full-time work. You are expected to accept a part-time job if you are offered one, unless it is accepted that you have a good reason for not doing so. You must normally take any job that pays at least the national minimum wage.

What the law says

Availability for work

You normally have to be available for any job of up to 35 hours a week that is within 90 minutes travel time (each way) of your home. You may be able to restrict your availability if:
- you have caring responsibilities for a child or a disabled person
- you have a health problem or disability
- you have a good work history (for the first three months of your claim)

Section 18 Welfare Reform Act 2012; regulations 88 and 97 The Universal Credit Regulations 2013

Do you have a good work history?

If you have been in work recently, you may be able to restrict the type of work you are seeking for up to three months after you claim. This includes both the type of job and the level of pay. The decision to allow you to restrict the sort of work that you are looking for is at the discretion of your personal adviser, who must accept that you have a reasonable chance of getting this kind of work. This rule also applies if you already get universal credit and you used to work and earn above your earnings threshold, but you have lost your job.

How your personal adviser might decide whether or not you can limit the jobs you look for is outlined in Box D.

Box D
Do you have a good work history?

Whether or not you can restrict the type of job you are looking may depend on:

- the availability of the type of job you used to do
- your prospects of getting the kind of job you used to have
- the length of time you were employed in the same occupation
- how long it has been since your last job ended
- your skills and qualifications
- training you have done for the job

Do you have childcare responsibilities?

If you are a lone parent or responsible carer of a child under 13, your availability for work is limited to be compatible with your child's normal school hours (including the time taken to travel to and from school).

Some children start school after their fifth birthday. If it is accepted as reasonable, you do not have to be available for work if you are the responsible carer of a child who is five and has not started school.

You may also be able to restrict your availability for work, if it is accepted that you have a reasonable prospect of finding work despite the restrictions. This could be allowed if you sometimes look after your child who normally lives with your ex-partner; or if your child is 13 or over but you need to look after her/him, perhaps as s/he has additional support needs.

Do you have a disability or health problems?

If you do not meet the conditions for having 'limited capability for work', but have a physical or mental impairment, you may be able to restrict your availability for work. You have to be available for the number of hours work that is considered to be reasonable, taking account of your impairment. If your impairment is accepted as having a substantial effect on your ability to carry out certain types of work, then you do not have to be available for this kind of work. You may be expected to provide evidence of how your condition or treatment limits the type, location or hours of work for which you are available. If you do not have to be available for full-time work, this also limits the number of hours you must spend looking for work.

If you are temporarily sick, you do not have to be available for work. You can only use this rule twice a year. You can 'self-certify' as sick for up to seven days, and provide a doctor's note for a further seven days after that. If you are sick for more than 14 days, you do not have to be available for work if the decision maker accepts that this is reasonable. You may be asked to provide medical evidence. If it is not accepted that you cannot be available for any work, you will need to try to limit the kind of work you are available for due to your health problems until you are assessed to see if you have 'limited capability for work'.

Do you care for a disabled person?

If you do not meet the conditions for having no work-related requirements due to your caring responsibilities, but you care for an ill or disabled person, you may be able to restrict your availability for work. As long as you are accepted as having a reasonable chance of finding work, you only have to be available for work that does not interfere with your caring responsibilities.

Do you already work?

If you work fewer hours than your claimant commitment says you must be available for work, you are expected to spend the rest of that time looking for more work, unless you are already earning enough to be above your 'earnings threshold'. This could be more work for your current employer, a second job or a different job with better pay.

You should not normally be expected to give up a permanent job for better paid, temporary work. In deciding whether it is reasonable for you to take another job, your personal adviser may take the length of the job into account, and also your other circumstances – eg, if your current job allows you to work flexibly because you have caring responsibilities.

Do you have to be available for work immediately?

You are normally expected to start work or attend a job interview immediately. There are some exceptions to this rule but you must still be willing and able to start work or attend an interview at the end of the extra time to benefit from them.

What the law says

Who does not need to be immediately available to attend an interview or start work?

- If you are employed, you *must* be given 48 hours' notice to attend an interview, and cannot be expected to take up a different job until the end of the notice period that you have to give for your current job.

- If you are doing voluntary work, you *may* be given up to 48 hours' notice to attend an interview and up to a week's notice to start paid work.

- If you have caring responsibilities for a child or disabled person, you *may* be given up to 48 hours' notice to attend an interview and a up to a month's notice to start work. This decision will take account of the alternative care arrangements that may be available to you.

Regulation 96 Universal Credit Regulations 2013

What does 'actively looking for work' mean?

You must normally spend the number of hours that your claimant commitment says you should be available for work actually looking for work. It must also be accepted that the action you take gives you the best chance of finding a job. The things you might be expected to do are explained in Box E.

Box E
Looking for work

You must be actively looking for work – ie, you must do anything reasonable to find a job. This may include spending time on specific activities such as:

- carrying out work searches
- applying for particular jobs
- maintaining an online profile

- registering with an employment agency
- cold-calling employers
- seeking references

You can also be asked to spend time preparing for work.

Keep as much evidence of what you have done to look for work as you can. This might include copies of application forms, letters from people you have contacted about jobs, or a written note of where you have dropped off CVs and who you have talked to about possible jobs. The more evidence you have, the more likely it is to be accepted that you have been looking for work.

EXAMPLE

Actively looking for work

Samantha has been claiming universal credit and looking for work for over six months. During this time she has registered with several employment agencies, and applied for specific jobs discussed with her presonal adviser. At a meeting to discuss Samantha's work-related requirements, her personal adviser decides that she needs to think about doing a training course to make her skills more attractive to employers.

While this is a work-preparation requirement, Samantha can be asked to do this as well. If it is accepted as reasonable by the adviser, she may not have to look for work while doing the course.

Are you working or volunteering?

If you already have a job, the hours that you spend at work should normally be deducted from the time you must spend looking for work each week. You are also allowed to deduct the time it takes you to travel to and from work.

If you are doing voluntary work, you can have the number of hours that you must spend looking for work reduced, if it is accepted that your volunteering gives you the best chance of finding paid work. However, the number of hours that you can spend volunteering instead of looking for work is limited to half of the hours that you are expected to spend looking for work.

For these rules to apply, the DWP must agree that you can reduce your hours of work search.

Are there any other special circumstances?

You do not have to look for work, although you may still be asked to take part in a work-focused interview or prepare for work, when:

- you have to attend court as party to a case or as a witness
- you are temporarily abroad for medical treatment (including treatment for your child)
- you are in treatment for drug or alcohol addiction for up to six months
- your partner or child, or the disabled person you cared for, has died within the last six months
- you are in prison

Your personal adviser can decide that you do not have to look for work while you are on a training course or doing other work preparation, if s/he accepts that it would be unreasonable for you to look for work as well. This will also apply if you are subject to any other temporary change of circumstances, as long as this is accepted as reasonable.

Your personal adviser can reduce or stop your work-related requirements temporarily, if you have done everything that it is reasonable to expect of you in a particular week, but you have not spent enough time looking for work. This rule might apply if you are moving house, or your child has been suspended from school, for example.

What CPAG says

Work-related requirements

CPAG has always welcomed the provision of support for benefit claimants to move into work if they are able to do so. However, the focus on the individual behaviour of claimants ignores barriers like the lack of secure jobs and the fact that work is not a guaranteed route out of poverty.

The claimant commitment is designed so that it sets out what work-related requirements a claimant has to meet. CPAG is concerned that the way in which the law has been written focuses on people complying with the rules. This is a missed opportunity to find a better way of engaging people in the process of moving towards work.

Another concern is that it will be harder to challenge decisions effectively if there is not a clear set of rules setting out when people can and cannot be expected to take certain action. This is likely to impact most on vulnerable groups who struggle to access advice and support to challenge decisions. Whatever the rules look like, it is vital that any decisions can be challenged by claimants on a level playing field.

One alternative to work-related requirements would be a 'personal budget' for moving towards work, which a claimant would decide how to spend in discussion with an adviser. Larger budgets could be allocated to people with health problems, a disability or caring responsibilities, in recognition of the extra barriers to work they face. This would allow the adviser to work with claimants, rather than dictating what they should do. It would also mean that the services that people use would be the right ones for their individual circumstances.

Further information

There is more information on the work-related requirements that apply to universal credit in CPAG's *Welfare Benefits and Tax Credits Handbook*.

Chapter 6
Sanctions and fines

This chapter covers:

1. When can your universal credit be sanctioned?

2. When is your universal credit not sanctioned?

3. How much is a sanction and how long does it last?

4. When can you get hardship payments?

5. When can you be fined?

6. What happens to your universal credit after a benefit offence?

What you need to know

- If you do not meet the conditions in your 'claimant commitment', the amount of your universal credit can be reduced. This is called being 'sanctioned'. The amount depends on why you are being sanctioned. The sanction can last indefinitely or for a set period. You should not be sanctioned if you have a good reason.

- If you cannot meet your essential needs because your universal credit is being sanctioned, you may be able to get a 'hardship payment'. This is a loan, which you may have to repay from your future universal credit.

- If you are overpaid universal credit because you fail to provide or give incorrect information, you may be given a 'civil penalty'.

- If you give false information or act dishonestly in relation to your universal credit claim and it is serious enough that there could be grounds to prosecute you for fraud, you may be able to accept a fine instead of being prosecuted. This is called a 'penalty as an alternative to prosecution'.

1. When can your universal credit be sanctioned?

If you do not meet your 'work-related requirements', your universal credit can be reduced. This is called being 'sanctioned'. The amount of the sanction and how long it lasts depends on whether or not you have to look for work as part of your work-related requirements and the reason for the sanction. A sanction should not be imposed if you can show 'good reason' for acting as you did.

Do you have to look for work?

If you have to look for work as a condition of getting universal credit, you can be sanctioned if, for example, you do not do something that is set out in your 'claimant commitment'. There are three levels of sanctions: high, medium and low.

What the law says

Sanctions if you have to look for work

You can be given a **high level** sanction if:
- you do not apply for a particular job
- you do not take up a job offer
- you do not take up a work placement
- you give up a job or lose pay voluntarily or because of misconduct

You can be given a **medium level** sanction if:
- you are not available to start work immediately
- you are not doing enough to find work

You can be given a **low level** sanctions if:
- you do not undertake any of your other work-related requirements, such as updating your CV
- you do not report a change of circumstances, provide information or attend an interview relevant to your work-related requirements

Sections 26 and 27 Welfare Reform Act 2012; regulations 102, 103 and 104
The Universal Credit Regulations 2013

EXAMPLES

Sanctions if you must look for work

Mandy lives alone and has no health problems. She gives up her job because she finds it boring. Two weeks later, she has not found work and she claims universal credit.

The decision maker at the Department for Work and Pensions (DWP) does not accept that Mandy had a good reason for leaving her job and decides that her universal credit will be sanctioned for 91 days.

Sanctions if you do not report a change of circumstances

Boris and Sonya claim universal credit as a couple. Sonya's daughter from her first marriage, Rhea, normally lives with them. Rhea is three years old so Sonya only has to attend work-focused interviews.

Rhea goes to live full time with her father. If Sonya does not immediately tell the Jobcentre Plus about the change in her circumstances, she may be sanctioned. This is because her work-related requirements will change as she is no longer Rhea's main carer and she may now be expected to look for work. She may also be overpaid universal credit if she does not report that her daughter no longer lives with her.

What if you do not have to look for work?

Even if you do not have to look for work, you can be sanctioned if you do not do something that is set out in your 'claimant commitment'. There are two levels of sanction: low and lowest.

What the law says

Sanctions if you do not have to look for work

You can be given a **low level** sanction if you are expected to prepare for work. You might be given a sanction if you:
- do not take up a work placement you are told to do
- do not undertake any of the activities that you are required to do to prepare for work
- do not take part in an interview to discuss your work-related requirements
- do not report a change in your circumstances that affects your work-related requirements

You can be given a **lowest level** sanction if you are expected to attend work-focused interviews (but have no other work-related requirements). You might be given a sanction if you:
- do not attend or participate in a work-focused interview
- do not report a change of circumstances relevant to your work-related requirements
- do not attend an interview relevant to your work-related requirements

Section 27 Welfare Reform Act 2012; regulations 104 and 105 Universal Credit Regulation 2013

How much is deducted from your benefit and how long the sanction lasts is explained in this chapter.

2. When is your universal credit not sanctioned?

In most cases, if you can show that you had a 'good reason' for acting as you did, your universal credit will not be reduced – ie, you will not be 'sanctioned'. What good reason means is not defined in the rules but there is guidance about the kinds of circumstances that may be taken into account (see Box A). As well as these general factors, there may be others more specific to the circumstances that led to the sanction. For example, it may be a good reason not to apply for a job if the amount you would have to pay in childcare or travel is an unreasonably high proportion of the pay.

Decision makers at the DWP should consider all your circumstances and have the discretion to decide whether you have a good reason. When making this decision, the decision maker is likely to use information from your personal adviser, as s/he may have referred you for a decision on whether you should be sanctioned. Make sure you give your own explanation too.

Box A
Do you have a good reason?

The following may be relevant when deciding whether or not you have a good reason:

- there is a domestic emergency
- you have a mental health condition
- you have a disability
- you have learning disabilities
- there would be significant harm to health
- there would be a risk to your health and safety or someone else's
- there would be unreasonable physical or mental stress
- you are homeless
- you have experienced domestic violence
- you have experienced bullying or harassment
- you have caring responsibilities
- you have a sincere religious or conscientious objection

EXAMPLE

Good reason

Terry is made redundant after doing the same job for 15 years. At an interview just after he claims universal credit, his personal adviser suggests that he should apply for a similar job with a different employer, which is being advertised through the jobcentre. Terry agrees to do this, as it sounds like a good opportunity.

Before applying, Terry contacts the employer for more details. The job is not based at the main office, which would mean Terry would be working a long way from home. He would have to travel for about two hours to get to work, and the train and bus fares would cost him almost half of the salary on offer. Terry explains this to his personal adviser and it is accepted that he has a good reason for not applying for the job.

Have you left work or lost earnings voluntarily or because of misconduct?

What the law says

When you should not be sanctioned

You should not be sanctioned if you:
- are made redundant or take voluntary redundancy
- leave or lose pay as a member of the armed forces, even if you left voluntarily
- have been laid off or put on short-time working by your employer
- leave a job or lose pay while still in a trial period
- are involved in a trade dispute
- leave a job or lose pay but your weekly earnings do not fall below the 'earnings threshold' set out in your claimant commitment

Regulation 113 Universal Credit Regulations 2013

If you leave your job or change your hours so that you lose earnings, you may be sanctioned. You should only be sanctioned if you have either done this voluntarily without a good reason or it has happened because of your misconduct.

The words 'voluntarily' and 'misconduct' are not defined in any special way. Box B highlights some issues to bear in mind.

Box B
What is 'misconduct'?

- Being careless or negligent might be misconduct if it is serious enough.

- Misconduct must normally be connected with your employment in some way, although it does not necessarily need to happen while you are working.

- Dishonesty is clearly misconduct if it means that your employer does not trust you and dismisses you because of this.

- Being persistently late or being off sick without explaining the situation to your employer might be misconduct.

- Refusing to work overtime might be misconduct if it is in your contract and the request was reasonable.

- If you resign to avoid being dismissed, this can count as misconduct.

- If you refuse to do something at work, this might be misconduct if you understood the instruction and do not have a good reason for refusing.

- If your employer says you were dismissed because of misconduct, but is really just reducing staff numbers, this should not count as misconduct.

- If you are dismissed for poor performance, this is not necessarily misconduct.

3. How much is a sanction and how long does it last?

If you are sanctioned, the most your universal credit can be reduced by is the amount of the adult 'standard allowance' that applies to you in your monthly award. If you are claiming as a couple and only one of you is sanctioned, the maximum reduction is half of your standard allowance as a couple.

You can be sanctioned for an indefinite period or a set number of days. A sanction starts from the beginning of the monthly assessment period in which you are sanctioned.

How much is a sanction?

As the length of a sanction is a particular number of days, the amount of the sanction is also worked out on a daily basis. The amount depends on whether you are single or a couple, and whether you are over or under 25.

For each day in the sanction, the amount in the table that applies to you is deducted from your universal credit award.

Daily rate of sanction		
	Usual rate	Lower rate
	£ per day	£ per day
Single		
Under 25	8.10	3.20
5 or over	10.20	4.00
Couple (per person sanctioned)		
Both under 25	6.30	2.50
Either 25 or over	8.00	3.20

Usually, the amount of the sanction (the usual rate) is the same as the amount of the standard allowance that is used to calculate your universal credit if you are single, and half the standard allowance (at the couple rate) if you are claiming jointly as a couple. When the sanction applies for the whole month, it may be that the daily amount works out at a bit more than the monthly standard allowance – eg, if there are 31 days in the month. In this case, the reduction will not be any more than the monthly standard allowance.

However, the **lower rate** applies instead if you are:

- given a 'lowest level' sanction
- aged 16 or 17
- the responsible carer of a child under one (and so you have no work-related requirements)
- pregnant and the baby is expected within 11 weeks, or you have had a baby in the last 15 weeks (and so you have no work-related requirements)

It is possible that the amount of the sanction is the same as or more than the amount of your universal credit award. In this case, you are paid no universal credit for the period of the sanction.

When you are sanctioned, you may find you are left without enough to pay for food and bills. You can apply for a hardship payment. These are explained on page 95.

EXAMPLE

The amount of a sanction

Duncan is 43, single and unemployed. His adviser notifies him of a job vacancy but Duncan does not apply for it because his mother is taken into hospital that day. He is sanctioned for 91 days. The sanction is applied for the whole of his monthly assessment periods for April, May and June. His usual universal credit award is £611.55 a month made up of £311.55 standard allowance and £300 housing costs. The sanction is £306 in April and June (30 days x £10.20) and £311.55 for May (31 days x £10.20, limited to the amount of his standard allowance). He gets paid about £300 a month for those three months, just enough to cover his rent but not enough for bills or food. Duncan does three things.

- He contacts his adviser to explain his reasons for not applying for the vacancy.
- He asks an advice centre for help to appeal against the sanction.
- He applies for a hardship payment.

How long does a sanction last?

The number of days a sanction lasts depends on the level of sanction and whether you have been sanctioned before. Sometimes the sanction lasts until you comply – ie, until you meet the requirement rather than for a set period.

Length of sanctions

Level of sanction	Length of sanction		
	First failure	Second failure within a year	Third failure within a year
High level eg, failure to apply for a job	91 days	182 days	1,095 days
Medium level eg, failure to take all reasonable action to get work	28 days	91 days	91 days
Low level eg, failure to take particular work preparation action	Until you comply plus seven days after that	Until you comply plus 14 days after that	Until you comply plus 28 days after that
Lowest level eg, failure to attend a work-focused interview	Until you comply	Until you comply	Until you comply

Shorter periods apply to 16- and 17-year-olds who are sanctioned.

EXAMPLE

Length of sanction

Jerry has limited capability for work and so his work-related requirements are that he is expected to prepare for work. He gets a low level sanction because he did not attend a training course his adviser found for him and he did not have a good reason for failing to attend. This is the first time Jerry has been sanctioned.

Jerry and his personal adviser agree that if he attends a different course, he will be treated as having met the original requirement and his sanction will end a week after he starts the course.

If you are already being sanctioned and you get another sanction, the new sanction will start when the current one ends. This means that the highest amount you are sanctioned for failing to meet your work-related requirements is still your full personal allowance, but a second sanction will mean you are sanctioned for longer. However, the total of all sanctions that currently apply to you can never be more than 1,095 days.

What happens if your circumstances change?

The sanction period continues even if your universal credit award ends. If you reclaim universal credit before the sanction period ends, the sanction continues for the remainder of the period.

If, since the start of your last sanction, you are in work for 26 weeks and earning above a certain amount, then any remaining sanctions on your universal credit award are written off. The amount you need to earn for this to apply is your 'earnings threshold', which is set out in your claimant commitment. Weeks in different jobs with gaps in between can count towards the 26 weeks.

The daily amount of a sanction is reduced to zero (ie, you will get your full universal credit entitlement) if you become unwell and move into the group with no work-related requirements, because you are accepted as having a limited capability for work and work-related activity. What this means is explained in Chapter 3. The sanction period will continue, so that if your health improves before the sanction period ends, the sanction can start again.

EXAMPLE

Continuation of sanction

Belle receives a high level sanction of 182 days because she left her job voluntarily and then failed to take up an offer of a suitable new job within a year. Eight weeks (56 days) after the start of the sanction period she gets a new job and her earnings mean that she no longer qualifies for universal credit so her award stops. However, Belle's new job ends after three months (92 days) as the company goes into administration, and she reclaims universal credit immediately. Her new award of universal credit will continue to be sanctioned until 182 days after the sanction period first started.

4. When can you get hardship payments?

If the amount of your universal credit is reduced because of a sanction, you may be able to get a 'hardship payment'. These are loans and are usually recovered from your universal credit.

To get a hardship payment of universal credit, you must be unable to meet your immediate 'essential needs' as a result of being sanctioned. If you are 16 or 17, you cannot get hardship payments as sanctions cannot reduce your universal credit by the full standard allowance. It is important to explain your circumstances when you apply. The DWP is more likely to accept that you need a hardship payment if, for example, you have children or caring responsibiltiies, or you are ill or pregnant. You can appeal if you are refused a hardship payment.

What the law says

What are essential needs?

Essential needs are:
- accommodation
- heating
- food
- hygiene

You should be able to meet immediate needs for yourself, your partner and your children. If you cannot, you may get a hardship payment.

Regulation 116 The Universal Credit Regulations 2013

Before you can get a hardship payment, you may need to show that you have tried to access other sources of support to meet your essential needs, such as discretionary housing payments or help from relatives. You may also have to show that you have tried to stop spending on anything other than those essential needs.

To get hardship payments, you must make an application and provide any required information as well as continue to meet your work-related requirements.

How much are hardship payments and how long do they last?

Hardship payments are paid at 60 per cent of the amount by which your universal credit has been reduced. For example, if you are a single person over 25 who is sanctioned for seven days so that your monthly universal credit payment is reduced by £71.40, the maximum hardship payment you can get before your next normal universal credit payment is due is £42.84.

Normally, a hardship payment is paid until your next universal credit payment is due. You then need to apply again the following month – ie, for each new monthly assessment period.

When do you pay back hardship payments?

Once the sanction period is over, you normally start to pay back the hardship payment. This is usually by having your universal credit award reduced until the hardship payment is repaid (in the same way as if you were paying back an overpayment of universal credit – see Chapter 7). However, sometimes you do not need to pay it back at all or for a period.

- You do not pay back a hardship payment while you are working and earning above a certain amount (this is your 'earnings threshold' which is set out in your claimant commitment).

- If you are in work and earning above that threshold for 26 weeks, any hardship payment not yet repaid is written off completely.

> **EXAMPLE**
>
> **Hardship payments**
>
> Anita and Tony have two children, aged six and eight. Tony has just resigned from his job and the couple have claimed universal credit. Tony is sanctioned for leaving his job without good reason. He is 'signing on' and looking for work. Anita is seven months' pregnant and unwell because of complications in her pregnancy. The couple have no other income. They explain their circumstances to the decision maker and provide evidence that they cannot meet their essential needs, have no non-essential expenditure and have not been able to get help from other members of their family. The decision maker decides that they can get a hardship payment of universal credit.
>
> Tony finds a new job which pays more than his universal credit earnings threshold. Recovery of the hardship payments they received is suspended, and once Tony has been working for 26 weeks, they are written off.
>
> Note that Tony is also able to appeal against the decision to sanction. He could argue that his wife's pregnancy and illness, together with the needs of their children, are good reasons for leaving his job (if this was why he stopped work).

5. When can you be fined?

There are two types of fines that you can receive when you are getting universal credit.

- A 'civil penalty' if you are overpaid universal credit because of something that you have done.

- A 'penalty as an alternative to prosecution' if the DWP thinks there may be grounds to prosecute you for fraud.

Seek advice immediately if you are being prosecuted for benefit fraud, have been offered a fine to avoid the possibility of being prosecuted, or have been invited to attend a formal interview.

When can you be given a civil penalty?

A civil penalty of £50 can be added to an overpayment of universal credit of £65.01 or more if the overpayment was caused by:

- your negligently making an incorrect statement
- your negligently providing incorrect information or evidence
- your failing to report a relevant change of circumstances 'without reasonable excuse'

In the first two cases, you are not given a penalty if you have taken 'reasonable steps' to correct your error.

Decision makers have discretion about when you are given a civil penalty and can decide whether you have been 'negligent' or have taken 'reasonable steps' to correct an error. For example, you might not be given a civil penalty at all if you have a mental health problem and you did not understand what you were doing, even if you have been overpaid.

You can only be given a civil penalty if you have not been charged with an offence or given a fine as an alternative to being prosecuted in connection with the same overpayment.

If you are given a civil penalty but do not think you were negligent, you think you had a reasonable excuse or think any overpayment was not worked out correctly, you may be able to appeal the decision.

EXAMPLE

Fines

Nigel works part time. His daughter Clara attends nursery while he works and he receives help towards the costs of childcare in his universal credit. Nigel decides he wants to spend more time with Clara, reorganises his work and reduces her childcare by a few hours a week. He mistakenly reports the wrong amount of childcare costs for two months. The decison maker decides that Nigel has been negligent, but that the situation is not sufficiently serious to prosecute him for fraud. Nigel's universal credit award is amended, an overpayment of £180 is calculated and a £50 fine is added to it.

Nigel can appeal against the decision to add a fine to his overpayment if he has a reasonable excuse for not informing the DWP earlier.

When can you be given a penalty as an alternative to prosecution?

If the DWP thinks that there are grounds for prosecuting you for a benefit fraud offence, you can be offered a penalty as an alternative to being prosecuted. If you accept the fine, you cannot be prosecuted for the same offence.

You have 14 days after accepting the fine to change your mind and withdraw your acceptance. If you withdraw your acceptance, the DWP must refund any of the fine you have already paid, but may decide to prosecute you instead.

If you accept a penalty as an alternative to prosecution, the amount you are fined is:

- £350 if there has been no overpayment
- 50 per cent of the overpayment, subject to a minimum of £350 and a maximum of £2,000

It may be difficult to decide what to do. On the one hand, if you accept the fine, you avoid prosecution. On the other hand, you will have to pay the fine and your universal credit will be sanctioned for a period. Always seek independent advice to help you decide.

EXAMPLE

Fine instead of a possible prosecution

Aaron claims universal credit for himself and his two children. Before any payment is made, his claim is turned down as the decision maker believes the children live with his ex-wife Maria, who already gets universal credit for them. Aaron has not provided any evidence of when the children stay with him. Even though no overpayment has been made to Aaron, the DWP believes that he deliberately claimed for the children dishonestly in order to get more benefit, and so he could be prosecuted for fraud. Rather than start proceedings, Aaron is offered the alternative of paying a £350 fine. He has 14 days in which to decide whether or not to accept it. He should seek advice.

Note that Aaron may also be able to argue that he can claim for the children, depending on their living arrangements. To be convicted, it must be proved that he knew he was not entitled to amounts of universal credit for them.

How do you pay a fine?

A fine is recoverable from you in the same way as an overpayment. There is more information about overpayments and how they are recovered in Chapter 7.

If you have a joint universal credit claim, the fine will be recovered from your joint award. It may also be recovered by other methods (eg, deductions from other benefits or from earnings) from you or from your partner. The fine will not be imposed on your partner if s/he was unaware of your negligence or if s/he has a reasonable excuse for not providing the information needed.

If a fine is being recovered from you and the decision that you have been overpaid is later changed (eg, if your appeal against the decision is successful), the DWP must refund any amount of the fine that you have already paid.

6. What happens to your universal credit after a benefit offence?

If you are convicted of a benefit offence or you accept a fine to avoid possible prosecution, your universal credit entitlement is sanctioned for a set period of time. This usually means that you are paid less benefit but, in some cases, this can mean losing entitlement altogether. You can apply for hardship payments.

The sanction lasts for four weeks if you accept a penalty as an alternative to prosecution. If you are convicted of a first offence, the sanction usually lasts for 13 weeks. If you are convicted again for another benefit offence, the sanction is longer.

What CPAG says

Sanctions and fines

CPAG does not agree with tougher sanctions for people who do not comply with the imposed work-related requirements.

There is little evidence that sanctions are an effective way to get people into sustainable jobs, or to reduce poverty rates overall. Furthermore, sanctions have been shown to have serious negative consequences. They are poorly understood by the people receiving them, who often do not know why their benefit has been reduced. They have a negative impact on health outcomes, and on poverty rates for individuals and families affected by them. Perhaps most worrying of all, research has shown that vulnerable groups are more likely to be sanctioned.

While the popular perception is one of 'scroungers' taking what they know they are not entitled to, CPAG fears that fines may be offered to frightened vulnerable people, who have made an innocent mistake. It is concerning that penalties have been introduced when there is no question that a person has acted dishonestly, or when someone has not actually been overpaid.

EXAMPLE

Sanction for a benefit offence

Connor accepts a fine of 50 per cent of the amount of an overpayment of universal credit as an alternative to being prosecuted, after it was found that he had not declared the casual work he had been doing. As well as the fine, he is sanctioned for four weeks.

Further information

You can look up official guidance about hardship payments in the DWP's *Advice for Decision Making* at www.dwp.gov.uk/publications/specialist-guides/advice-for-decision-making/.

There is more information about fraud and penalties in CPAG's *Welfare Benefits and Tax Credits Handbook*.

Chapter 7
Dealing with universal credit problems

This chapter covers:

1. What can you do if there is a problem with your universal credit?

2. What happens if you are overpaid?

3. What can you do if you disagree with a decision?

4. Making a complaint

What you need to know

- If you are overpaid universal credit, the Department for Work and Pensions (DWP) can recover it, even if its own mistake caused the overpayment.

- Decision makers have discretion not to recover an overpayment.

- If the DWP decides to recover an overpayment, you do not have a right of appeal against this. However, you may be able to challenge the decision in other ways.

- The DWP will usually recover an overpayment from your ongoing award of universal credit, but may recover it in other ways, including from your earnings.

- With most decisions about universal credit, if you are unhappy you can appeal to an independent tribunal. Before you do so, you will need to ask the DWP to consider revising the decision.

1. What can you do if there is a problem with your universal credit?

Various problems can arise with your universal credit award or payment. What you can do about the problem depends on what has gone wrong.

- If your circumstances have changed, you must report anything that might affect your benefit or any other change you are told to report as soon as possible. There is more information about changes in circumstances in Chapter 4.

- If you are told that you have been overpaid universal credit, you may have to repay it. First, you should check whether the overpayment is correct.

- If you are unhappy with your award, you can ask the Department for Work and Pensions (DWP) to change the decision, and if you are still unhappy, you can appeal.

- If there is a delay in getting paid, you may be able to get a 'short-term advance'. There is more information on these payments in Chapter 4.

- If your benefit is reduced because of a 'sanction', you can ask the DWP to change the decision, and if you are still unhappy, you can appeal. There is more information about sanctions in Chapter 6.

- If you are fined, you can ask the DWP to change the decision, and if you are still unhappy, you can appeal. There is more information about fines in Chapter 6.

2. What happens if you are overpaid?

If more universal credit is paid to you than you are entitled to, you have been overpaid.

There are many reasons why universal credit might be overpaid, including the following.

- You give the wrong information when you claim.

- You are late reporting a change of circumstances.

- Your employer gives the wrong details about your earnings when reporting these to HM Revenue and Customs (HMRC).

- The DWP makes a mistake when it works out your award or when it records information you give.

- The DWP does not act on information you give.

- The DWP does not pass on information from one department to another.

EXAMPLES

Why overpayments happen

Parveen is working part time. Her employer has mixed up the details of her earnings with those of someone else and has told HMRC that she earns less than she does. When the mistake comes to light, the DWP revises her award. She has an overpayment of universal credit.

Jerry claims universal credit when he stops work because of cancer treatment. His partner moves in to look after him. He does not realise he needs to tell the DWP. When he does tell the DWP some months later, he finds he has an overpayment of universal credit as they should have claimed as a couple.

Anna has an award of universal credit of £300 a month. One month, there is a mix-up in the system and two sums of £300 are paid into her bank account on the same day by mistake. Anna queries it and is told that this is an overpayment.

If your universal credit is overpaid, the DWP should do the following.

- **Change the decision.** If the overpayment is because of a change in your entitlement to universal credit, the DWP usually must 'revise' or 'supersede' the decision awarding you benefit. These are the legal ways in which the DWP can change a decision on your entitlement. In some circumstances, the DWP does not have to change the decision before recovering an overpayment – eg, if you are paid twice by mistake or if someone else receives a payment intended for you.

- **Calculate the overpayment.** Normally this is the difference between what you were actually paid and how much you were properly entitled to.

- **Decide whether to recover the overpayment.** By law, any overpayment is recoverable even if it is not your fault. However, the decision whether or not to recover the overpayment is at the decision maker's discretion.

- **Decide from whom to recover the overpayment.** The general rule is that an overpayment can be recovered from the person to whom it was paid. If you claim jointly as a couple, it can be recovered from one or both of you, even if you are not the one who received the payment.

- **Decide how to recover the overpayment.** There are various methods the DWP can use to recover an overpayment.

Do you have to pay back an overpayment?

What the law says

Repaying overpayments

The DWP is legally entitled to ask you to repay any overpayment, even if it was due to a DWP mistake. This means you cannot appeal against a decision to recover an overpayment.

Section 71ZB Social Security Administration Act 1992

According to the code of practice (see page 113), the DWP intends to ask for all overpayments to be paid back. In exceptional circumstances, the DWP may decide not to recover some or all of an overpayment. An example is where recovery could cause you or your family hardship and affect your health or welfare. The code of practice does not say an overpayment will be written off just because it was the DWP's mistake. You could still ask for this but also explain the effect on your family if you have to repay it.

Although you cannot appeal against a decision to recover an overpayment, if you think you should not have to pay back the overpayment, you can dispute it.

Box A

What can you do if you have been overpaid?

- If paying back the overpayment will cause you hardship or affect you or your family's health or welfare, ask for some or all of it to be written off. If it was the DWP's fault not yours, explain this too.

- If the DWP does not do as you ask, you can consider using its internal complaints procedure.

- If you are still unhappy, you can take your case to an Independent Case Examiner.

- Check your award carefully. If you disagree with the amount you have been overpaid, ask for this to be 'revised' and then appeal if the DWP does not revise it. This is different from disputing the recovery of the overpayment. You can do this at the same time as disputing recovery, but you need to make it clear that you are appealing against the amount of the overpayment and not whether it can be recovered.

- In exceptional cases, you could seek advice about making a legal challenge, called a 'judicial review'.

EXAMPLE

Disputing an overpayment

Marion has separated from her partner, Geoff, who has moved out of the family home. The relationship has been off and on for a while and Marion hoped he would be back. She is currently feeling depressed and anxious. Six months later, Marion tells the DWP that Geoff has gone. The DWP revises her universal credit award from the date that Geoff moved out and works out how much she has been overpaid. She is told that amounts to repay this overpayment will be deducted each month from her award. Marion thinks this will leave her with insufficient money on which to manage. She does three things.

- She checks her award and discovers the date the DWP has said Geoff moved out is a month too early. She asks the DWP to revise the award. When it refuses, she appeals.

- She asks the DWP to write off the overpayment because the repayments are causing her hardship and her mental ill health makes it very hard for her to deal with problems, including reporting changes that affect her universal credit at the right time.

- She seeks advice from an advice centre. This helps her check that the amount of the overpayment is correct, and helps her with the dispute and appeal.

How do you pay back an overpayment?

What the law says

Recovering overpayments

The DWP can recover overpayments of universal credit by:
- making deductions from an ongoing award of benefit you have
- reducing an amount of arrears of benefit that is owed to you
- making deductions from your earnings
- taking court action against you

Sections 105 and 108 Welfare Reform Act 2012; The Social Security (Overpayment and Recovery) Regulations 2013

The usual way of repaying an overpayment is from your ongoing award of benefit. This might be universal credit or it might be another benefit. Deductions can be made from most benefits, but not from child benefit or guardian's allowance. The maximum amount that can be deducted from your universal credit for an overpayment is normally 15 per cent of your standard allowance. However, it can be more than this if you have earnings, if fraud is involved or if it is hardship payments that are being recovered.

If you are employed, the DWP can recover overpayments of universal credit from your earnings. The DWP will send a notice to you and your employer to say how much is to be deducted. No deduction is made if your net earnings are less than £100 a week or £430 a month. You employer can also deduct a £1 administration charge from your earnings each time it makes a deduction for an overpayment.

The DWP can recover an overpayment of universal credit through the courts and might do so if it cannot recover in another way – eg, if you are not receiving any benefits and not working. Court costs can be added to the overpayment and treated as part of it. There are time limits in which the DWP needs to start court action. There is no time limit for recovering overpayments in other ways.

EXAMPLE

Repaying an overpayment

Mona has been getting universal credit as someone with limited capability for work, but starts a part-time job. Her award is adjusted. A year later, the DWP decides it has miscalculated her entitlement since she started working. Her award is reassessed and the amount she has been overpaid is worked out. The decision maker decides to recover the overpayment and to do so from both her ongoing universal credit award and her earnings, as her current award is low and the rate of recovery from her earnings will not cause her hardship. Her employer makes the deductions the DWP has requested from Mona's wages.

What CPAG says

Recovering overpayments

CPAG is concerned that a system in which all overpayments of universal credit are legally recoverable is unfair on claimants, particularly if the overpayment has arisen through no fault of their own. A discretionary system to decide when to write off an overpayment is no substitute for an independent right of appeal. With more overpayments being recovered from claimants than would be allowed under the current system, more people will be left in hardship.

3. What can you do if you disagree with a decision?

If you disagree with a decision about your universal credit, you can challenge it.

First you should ask the DWP to look at its decision again. This is called asking for a reconsideration (the legal term is 'revision'). A decision maker can revise a decision if you ask for this within a month of the date the decision was sent to you. If it has been longer than a month, a decision can still be revised if there are special reasons to extend the time limit, or if it can be revised or 'superseded' (another legal way to change a decision) on particular grounds.

If the DWP refuses to revise the decision or does revise it, it should send you a 'mandatory reconsideration notice' explaining your right of appeal if you are still not happy. You have a right of appeal against most decisions, but not about whether to recover an overpayment or what your work-related requirements are. Once you have this notice, you can then appeal to an independent appeal tribunal.

There are strict time limits on appealing. You should appeal within one month of being sent the mandatory reconsideration notice, although the time limits can be extended for special reasons.

EXAMPLE

Disagreeing with a decision

Ilona gets universal credit for herself and her child. She has mental health problems and has been getting an additional element in her award for being ill. At her next medical examination, she is assessed as being fit for work. She receives a decision saying that her universal credit award will no longer include the additional element. Ilona believes she is too ill to work and wants to challenge this. She is not sure how to do so and contacts the DWP to say she wants to appeal. Because the rules say she must first ask for a revision, the DWP treats this as a request to consider revising the decision. After reconsidering the decision, the DWP decides not to revise it. Ilona can now appeal. She makes her written appeal immediately so she does not miss the deadline, and seeks advice from her local advice centre to help make her case.

What CPAG says

Appealing decisions

The introduction of a new requirement for claimants to request a revision before being able to exercise their right of appeal adds further delays into an already lengthy process and potentially causes hardship. Some people with strong cases may be put off from properly exercising their appeal rights by having to go through the extra stage in the process.

4. Making a complaint

If you disagree with a decision on your universal credit award or payment, first check whether you can ask for this to be changed by using the 'revision' and appeal process. Box A outlines the action you can take if the DWP says you have been overpaid. If you are unhappy with the way your universal credit claim has been handled, you can make a complaint.

You may want to complain about:

- a delay in dealing with your claim
- poor administration in the DWP benefit office
- poor advice from the DWP
- poor administration or advice from the Work Programme provider helping you look for or prepare for work
- a poorly conducted DWP medical examination
- the way the system affects you

How do you complain about the Department for Work and Pensions?

If you are unhappy with the way your claim has been handled, you should first take this up with the office dealing with it. Contact details should be on any letters you have about your claim. If this does not resolve the issue, the DWP has a complaints procedure – this can be found on the www.gov.uk website. Once you have gone through all the steps in the complaints procedure, if you are still unhappy with the response, you can take your case to the Independent Case Examiner. Alternatively, you can contact your MP and ask her/him to refer your complaint to the Ombudsman.

How do you complain about a Work Programme provider?

If you are unhappy with the service, advice or administration from a Work Programme provider, you should first contact the provider. If you are not satisfied with the response once you have been through its own complaints procedure, you can complain to the Independent Case Examiner.

How do you complain about a medical examination?

DWP medical examinations are conducted by contracted providers such as Atos Healthcare. To complain about the conduct of a medical examination or about the healthcare professional who carried it out, initially contact the contracted provider and go through its complaints procedure. If you are not satisfied with the response, you can complain to the Independent Case Examiner.

How do you use your MP?

If you do not have a particular universal credit issue to resolve, but you are unhappy with the way the system affects you, you may wish to take this up with your local MP.

You can also take up a specific problem with your MP. Normally it is best to do this if you have already tried to resolve the problem directly with the DWP but are still dissatisfied. In particular, it can be useful to ask your MP for help if there has been a delay in your claim being dealt with.

You can email or write to your MP, or go to a local 'surgery' – ie, the regular sessions that MPs usually have to meet their constituents. To find out who your MP is and how to contact her/him, see http://findyourmp.parliament.uk. You can also find contact details in your local library or town hall, or you can write to your local MP at the House of Commons, London SW1A 0AA.

Further information

The DWP has produced a code of practice called *What happens if you are overpaid Universal Credit, Jobseeker's Allowance or Employment and Support Allowance?* (COP1) which is available at www.gov.uk.
For information and tactical tips on appeals, see CPAG's guide *Winning your benefit appeal: what you need to know.*

Atos Healthcare Customer Relations
Wing G, Government Buildings
Lawnswood
Leeds LS16 5PU
Tel: 0113 230 9175
email: customer-relations@atoshealthcare.com

Parliamentary and Health Service Ombudsman
Millbank Tower
Millbank
London SW1P 4QP
Tel: 0345 015 4033
www.ombudsman.org.uk

Independent Case Examiner
Jupiter Drive
Chester CH70 8DR
Tel: 0845 606 0777
Textphone: 0151 801 8888
Fax 0151 801 8825
email: ice@dwp.gsi.gov.uk
www.ind-case-exam.org.uk

Chapter 8
Moving onto universal credit

This chapter covers:

1. Timetable

2. Changes of circumstances

3. Moving from benefits to universal credit

4. Moving from tax credits to universal credit

5. Top-up payments

6. Universal credit and other financial help

What you need to know

- People will move onto universal credit at different times, according to their circumstances and the area in which they live.

- The process of moving everyone from the old benefits and tax credits system onto universal credit is not expected to be completed until the end of 2017.

- You cannot claim universal credit at the same time as receiving any of the means-tested benefits and tax credits it is replacing.

- You should not be worse off financially when you move onto universal credit.

- Receiving universal credit may mean you can get other financial help, such as health benefits, free school lunches for your children and Healthy Start vouchers.

1. Timetable

When can you claim universal credit?

New claims for universal credit began in April 2013 in one jobcentre only, with three more from July, all in selected areas of North West England. This is a pilot scheme, referred to by the Department for Work and Pensions (DWP) as the 'Pathfinder'. See Box A for more information.

From 28 October 2013, new claims for universal credit are possible in other areas nationwide, although it is being introduced gradually in one district per region. You can only claim when it has been introduced in the area in which you live.

However, new claims for universal credit are not possible while you or your partner are receiving any of the old means-tested benefits listed in Box B.

This chapter looks at when and how you can move onto universal credit if you have been getting one or more of the old benefits and tax credits. **Note:** this process is not yet finalised and most of the information in this chapter is taken from DWP briefings rather than the law.

Claimants are being moved onto universal credit in three phases.

BOX A
Pathfinder pilot

Pathfinder areas

The areas are specified postcodes in Ashton-under-Lyne from 29 April, then Oldham, Warrington and Wigan from July. Claimants in these areas who do not fall into the Pathfinder group can continue to claim the old benefits and tax credits during the pilot period.

Pathfinder group

In addition to the basic conditions for universal credit listed in Chapter 2, to be able to claim as part of the pilot in these areas, you must:

- be single without children
- be a British citizen who has lived in the UK for the last two years
- be aged over 18 and under 60 years and six months
- be fit for work
- not have capital of more than £6,000
- not be pregnant
- not be a carer for a disabled person
- not be earning more than £330 a month (£270 if you are under 25)
- not be self-employed
- not be a homeowner, homeless or in supported accommodation
- not be entitled to, or awaiting a decision or appeal about, any of the old benefits listed in Box B or the contributory versions of jobseeker's allowance or employment and support allowance, or disability living allowance or personal independence payment

The Pathfinder pilot involves a small number of claimants, mainly single people who are newly unemployed. If a single person getting universal credit in the Pathfinder pilot forms a couple with someone who does not meet the above conditions, they can claim universal credit as a couple. Once someone starts to get universal credit, s/he stays on universal credit even if s/he moves out of the Pathfinder area, or circumstances change.

Box B
Old benefits and tax credits

These means-tested benefits and tax credits are based on your circumstances and the amount of money you have. They are being abolished and replaced by universal credit:

- income support
- income-based jobseeker's allowance
- income-related employment and support allowance
- housing benefit

- child tax credit
- working tax credit

More details of the timetable for when and how universal credit will be introduced are expected in autumn 2013. When fully introduced for new claimants, you will not be able to make a new claim for any of these benefits or tax credits. Once on universal credit, you will not be able to move back onto old benefits and tax credits.

Phase one: 28 October 2013 to April 2014

Phase one is primarily aimed at jobseekers, who are the first to claim universal credit. From October 2013, universal credit is being introduced across all seven regions of Great Britain; Scotland, Wales, North West England, North East England, Central England, Southern England, London and Home Counties. Each region is divided into districts. Universal credit is being introduced in one district at a time per region, with the aim that it is available nationwide by mid-2014. The intention in this phase is that once universal credit is introduced in a district new claims for old means-tested benefits and tax credits are phased out for people who are unemployed. It is also planned that some claimants who have a change of circumstances that means they are no longer entitled to the old benefits or tax credits can also move onto universal credit during this phase. However, these plans are likely to change as the DWP learns lessons from the universal credit pathfinder.

Phase two: from 6 April 2014

Phase two includes new claims from people in work – eg, those who would have previously made a claim for tax credits. The intention in this phase is that all new claims across the UK, whether from people in or out of work, by mid-2014 will be for universal credit. It was also planned that other claimants whose circumstances change can claim universal credit in this phase instead of one of the old benefits or tax credits. For example, someone who has a new baby claims universal credit instead of child tax credit, and someone who becomes liable for rent claims universal credit instead of housing benefit, and entitlement to any other old benefits or tax credits will stop. However, this timetable is very much subject to change.

Phase three: autumn 2014 to end of 2017

Phase three consists of moving existing claimants whose circumstances have not changed onto universal credit. This final phase eventually covers all claimants receiving one or more of the old benefits, including those who are seen as furthest from the labour market, such as severely disabled people, who may have been getting the old benefits for several years. This also includes people with non-benefit income who are only getting housing benefit. Tax credit claims will gradually be stopped and people will be moved onto universal credit at any point during the year, rather than waiting for the end of a tax year, so that claims do not all end at the same time.

The timetable is very likely to change to take into account the results of the pilot, testing of IT systems, local caseloads and economic circumstances.

2. Changes of circumstances

Once universal credit has been introduced in your area, and new claims for the old benefits have been phased out, a change of circumstances may mean that you move onto universal credit. If you are getting one of the old benefits or tax credits and your, or your partner's, circumstances change in a certain way, you can claim universal credit. This happens if the change means your old benefit ends or you would previously have had to claim another benefit or tax credit which has been replaced by universal credit. This includes the following circumstances.

- You have your first baby, or become responsible for a child for the first time. You cannot claim child tax credit or any addition for a child in the old benefits, so you have to claim universal credit.

- You are getting income support as a lone parent and your youngest child reaches the age of five. You cannot claim income-based jobseeker's allowance, so you have to claim universal credit.

- You are found fit for work. Your employment and support allowance ends (after an appeal) and you cannot claim income-based jobseeker's allowance, so you have to claim universal credit.

- You become liable for rent. For example, if you are getting income support and move away from your parents and into rented accommodation, you cannot claim housing benefit anymore, so you need to claim universal credit.

- You start work. You can no longer claim working tax credit, so you need to claim universal credit. If you start working, entitlement to means-tested benefits does not automatically end, as it depends on your hours and earnings, but universal credit should be available for you to claim in most cases.

Remember, if you are in a couple and the change affects you or your partner, you need to make a joint claim for universal credit. Once you claim universal credit, entitlement to any of the old benefits for you or your partner ends. If your circumstances change again, it is not possible to go back to your old benefit.

In these cases, the amount of universal credit that you get is calculated according to your circumstances and income. There is no top-up payment as your old benefit has ended because of the change in circumstances. In these situations, the DWP will not automatically move you onto universal credit, you must make a claim.

EXAMPLE

Claiming universal credit after a change of circumstances

Larry and Peter are a couple. Peter is disabled and gets disability living allowance. Larry is his carer and gets carer's allowance. Larry claims income support as a carer, including for Peter as his partner, and housing benefit. In December 2013, Peter's disability living allowance runs out and he is informed that he is not entitled to personal independence payment. Larry's carer's allowance stops and he is no longer entitled to income support. Universal credit has been introduced in their area, so Larry cannot claim income-based jobseeker's allowance and Peter cannot claim income-related employment and support allowance. They must claim universal credit instead. The amount of universal credit does not relate to how much they were getting on income support.

3. Moving from benefits to universal credit

If you are getting one of the old benefits and your circumstances have not changed, the DWP will move you onto universal credit at some stage during Phase 3.

Your old benefit claim ends and you are moved onto universal credit. As the DWP already has all the information it requires to start the universal credit claim, this can happen automatically without your having to do anything. Your claim will be moved over, and you are under an obligation to notify any changes or whether there is anything incorrect about your new claim.

The amount that you get on universal credit should not be less than the total you were getting from your old benefit, housing benefit and child tax credit. In some cases it may work out to be more – but this is only likely to be the case if you are not disabled and are working under 16 hours a week. In some cases, the amount of universal credit works out as less than your old benefits – especially if you are severely disabled. In this case, you receive a top-up payment so that you are not worse off overall at the time that you move onto universal credit.

If you are getting a benefit for yourself, as well as housing benefit and child tax credit for your children, all claims will stop at the same time. You can request a short-term advance of universal credit to help you manage until your first payment is due.

Transferring on to universal credit

Catriona gets income support as a lone parent with one child born in April 2013. She also gets child tax credit and housing benefit. She is still eligible for income support until her child reaches the age of five. However, by mid-2015 she is one of only a handful of people still getting housing benefit in her area. The DWP and local authority decide to move everyone over to universal credit. The DWP writes to her to say that her claims will be transferred to universal credit on a certain date. She does not have to make a claim and she cannot appeal about the decision. Her income support, child tax credit and housing benefit claims are ended and she starts to receive universal credit. She applies for a short-term advance to help her budget until the first monthly payment comes through.

4. Moving from tax credits to universal credit

Child tax credit and working tax credit are being abolished and replaced by universal credit for new claimants from 6 April 2014 under current plans (although the timetable is subject to change). If you are already getting tax credits, HM Revenue and Customs will stop your claim at some point after this date and you will be moved onto universal credit. If you were claiming tax credits as a single person, and you become part of a couple with someone who is getting universal credit, your tax credit award ends and you can claim universal credit jointly as a couple.

You may be able to make a new claim for tax credits between October 2013 and 6 April 2014 (or the date from which claims from working age people are no longer accepted) if universal credit has not yet been introduced in your district, or if you were entitled to tax credits earlier in the year. Tax credits are usually assessed and paid based on your income during a complete tax year (6 April to 5 April). However, when you are moved onto universal credit, your tax credit claim may be stopped at any time during the year, rather than waiting until the end of the tax year. The intention is that your tax credit entitlement will be finalised according to your income for the part of the year up the point when you are moved onto universal credit. This will be the figure that is used to compare with your universal credit to decide whether you should receive a top-up payment. If you were entitled to a higher amount of tax credits than universal credit, you will be entitled to a top-up payment to ensure that you are not worse off at the point when you move onto universal credit.

There is no savings limit for tax credits, although interest or other payments from investments counts as income. You are not normally entitled to universal credit if you have more than £16,000 in savings. If you were getting tax credits and you had savings or other capital of over £16,000, the government has said that you will be entitled to universal credit under a special rule that protects your entitlement.

If you are getting tax credits and housing benefit, both claims will stop at the same time.

EXAMPLE

Moving from tax credits to universal credit

Bianca is a lone parent with two children and works an average of 30 hours a week on the minimum wage, with an annual salary of around £10,000. In 2013/14, her income is reduced to around £4,000 because she is on maternity leave. This means that in 2014/15, she starts to receive a higher amount of tax credits because her award uses her 2013/14 income. If she is moved onto universal credit in September 2014, her final tax credits entitlement is calculated according to her actual income in 2014/15. This means that her universal credit entitlement is compared with a lower tax credit amount when deciding whether she is entitled to a top-up payment.

5. Top-up payments

If you are moved from benefits or tax credits onto universal credit, you may receive a top-up payment to ensure that you do not lose out immediately. The circumstances where you are likely to receive a top-up payment include the following.

- You are entitled to the highest rate of the care component of disability living allowance or personal independence payment rate for daily living. An 'enhanced disability premium' was payable in income-based benefits, but this is not part of universal credit.

- You are entitled to the middle or higher rate of the care component of disability living allowance or personal independence payment rate for daily living, live alone and no one claims carer's allowance for looking after you. A 'severe disability premium' was payable in old benefits, but this is not part of universal credit.

- You have children and you have more than £16,000 in savings. You could still get child tax credit in this situation but you are normally be excluded from universal credit because of your savings.

- You have a disabled child who gets disability living allowance. The amount allowed for most disabled children in universal credit is significantly reduced, except for those on the highest rate of the care component.

- You are in work and you qualify for housing benefit with a 100 per cent disregard of your childcare costs from your earnings.

In these cases, it may not be in your interests to claim universal credit before you are moved onto it by the DWP. So, if there is a possibility that your circumstances may change so that your old benefit would stop and you have to claim universal credit, seek advice about how this affects you and whether you have any option of staying on your old benefit.

The amount of the top-up payment is calculated according to your full entitlement to the old benefit or tax credits, ignoring any sanctions or deductions, although these may continue to be made from your total universal credit.

If you are in work and your earnings rise, which means your universal credit goes down, the amount of the top-up payment is unaffected. If your earnings reach the point where you would be entitled to no universal credit, your top-up payment will then start to be withdrawn at a rate of 65 pence for every pound that you earn.

If your circumstances change so that you become entitled to a higher amount of universal credit, your top-up payment will stop if your new total is higher.

Your top-up payment will stop as a result of certain changes in circumstances. Once you have lost your top-up payment, you cannot get it back, even if your circumstances change again. The circumstances where you lose your top-up payment include:

- a partner leaves or joins the household
- a sustained (three-month) earnings drop beneath the level of work set out in your claimant commitment
- one (or both) members of the household stop work
- the universal credit award ends

However, if you are getting a top-up payment, your universal credit will be frozen. This means the total amount you receive, including the top-up payment, will not go up in April each year when other rates of universal credit, benefits and tax credits increase. Once the basic amount of universal credit catches up with the total that you receive, then you will start to receive universal credit as normal and you will no longer get a top-up payment.

EXAMPLE

Topping up universal credit payments

Sami is severely disabled and lives alone, getting personal independence payment at the enhanced rate for daily living. He is getting income-related employment and support allowance of £181.15 a week including the support component, enhanced disability premium and severe disability premium. He gets housing benefit of £80 a week. This is a total of £261.15 a week, which works out as £1,131.65 a month.

Under universal credit, he is entitled to £311.55 a month as a single person, plus £303.66 for limited capability for work-related activity, and £346.66 a month for rent. This is a total of £961.87 a month. When he is moved onto universal credit, Sami is entitled to a top-up payment of £169.78 a month so that the total he receives is £1,131.65 a month, the same as he was getting on the old benefits. This amount will not increase for several years. If a partner moves in, or he goes abroad for more than the allowed period, or he earns enough to come off universal credit for a while, he will lose entitlement to the top-up payment. If he needs to reclaim universal credit as a single person in future, he would get the basic universal credit amount of £961.87 a month with no top-up payment.

6. Universal credit and other financial help

If you get universal credit, you are eligible (if you pass the other qualifying conditions) for a:

- Sure Start maternity grant (a £500 grant to help with the costs of a newborn baby, usually just for a first baby)
- funeral expenses payment (covers basic funeral costs)
- cold weather payment (for weeks of below freezing weather)

Under the old system, if you get certain income-related benefits, such as income support, income-based jobseeker's allowance, income-related employment and support allowance or child tax credit, you qualify for other financial help. This is known as 'passporting'.

Other financial help includes:

- free prescriptions in England
- free NHS sight tests and glasses in England and Wales
- free dental treatment
- fares to hospital
- Healthy Start vouchers
- free school lunches
- school clothing grants

- help with heating and energy efficiency measures
- legal aid
- local leisure facility discounts
- social tariffs from utility companies

Some schemes are administered by central government departments, some by the Scottish and Welsh governments, and some by local authorities or other agencies. Some of this passported help is provided in cash or vouchers and some by discounts on charges. In general, you must make a separate claim for the passported help. In some cases, you must receive the necessary out-of-work benefit to qualify and people not getting the required benefit but who are on a low income are excluded. As universal credit is introduced and these benefits are abolished, the old criteria must change.

The government intends to maintain eligibility for those who would have qualified under the old system.

Passporting

Some universal credit claimants are automatically entitled to other types of financial help. For people in the Pathfinder pilot scheme, receipt of universal credit is a passport to exemption from NHS costs and to free school lunches. This is so that people who would previously have claimed income-based jobseeker's allowance do not lose this extra financial help because they get universal credit instead. However, they can still get this help if they start work, as long as they still receive universal credit. Note that the Pathfinder pilot only involves claimants without children, but if their circumstances change so that they become responsible for a school-age child, they would remain on universal credit and become entitled to free school lunches. The criteria in the longer term has not been set at the time of writing, and may involve an income threshold, although this would add another layer of complexity.

Other help when starting work

The old system included various other payments that were designed to act as an incentive on starting work. These included:

- in-work credit for lone parents
- return-to-work credit for disabled people
- job grant
- extended payments of housing benefit
- childcare disregard in housing benefit
- disregard of increase in income for tax credits

These payments are being phased out and there is no specific equivalent in universal credit. The value of these payments is often forgotten when comparing universal credit with the old system.

What CPAG says

Free school lunches

Passporting may evolve in the future to a more automated processes for claiming and receiving free school lunches or some types of other financial help, which could be paid as part of universal credit. However, it is hoped that the precedent set in the pilot of free school lunches if in receipt of any universal credit will not be reversed, as anything less or the introduction of an income threshold or taper will undermine the guiding principles of simplification and making work pay. Ultimately, universal free school lunches is the simplest system, and the best way to avoid work disincentives, as well as ensuring healthy nutritious meals for all schoolchildren.

Chapter 9
Universal credit and specific groups of people

This chapter highlights the impact of universal credit on the following groups of people:

1. Lone parents

2. Carers

3. Disabled people

4. Older people

5. People from abroad

6. Young people

What you need to know

- You do not need to be in any specific group to be entitled to universal credit. However, your circumstances determine what conditions apply to you and how much you can get.

- The 'work-related requirements' that lone parents must meet to get universal credit vary, depending on the age of their youngest child.

- Full-time carers have no work-related requirements and may be entitled to an additional amount of universal credit.

- Disabled people must have a medical assessment of their ability to work or to prepare for work. They may have no work-related requirements, or some or all requirements, depending on the extent of their disability. Some may qualify for an additional amount.

- People over the qualifying age for pension credit cannot claim universal credit and must still claim pension credit. If one member of a couple reaches the qualifying age for pension credit and the other is of working age, they must claim universal credit.

- Certain people from abroad are excluded from universal credit.

- Special rules allow some 16/17-year-olds and some young people in education to claim universal credit.

1. Lone parents

Can lone parents claim universal credit?

Lone parents can claim universal credit. You are a lone parent if you are responsible for a child who normally lives with you and you do not have a partner living with you.

If you are a lone parent, you make a single claim for universal credit, but you must make a joint claim as a couple if you have a partner living with you. It is important to be clear about whether you are a lone parent and be aware that if a partner moves in with you, even if s/he is not the parent of your child, you become a couple and will have a joint universal credit award.

Are there any special rules for lone parents?

If you are a lone parent, the maximum amount of universal credit payable to you is based on an allowance for yourself and your children, plus an amount for housing costs and, if you are in work, an amount for your childcare costs. There are additional amounts if you care for a disabled child or adult, or if you or your child are disabled.

There is no additional amount specifically for lone parents, but there are special rules that are aimed at providing a greater work incentive for lone parents. The 'work allowance', which is the amount you can earn before your universal credit is reduced, is higher for lone parents than for some other groups.

There is more information on how universal credit is calculated in Chapter 3.

If you share care with a former partner, it is not possible to split payments for children. You can agree who should claim for the child or, if you cannot agree, the Department for Work and Pensions (DWP) will decide which one of you has the main responsibility. This does not automatically go to who claimed first, or who gets child benefit, but takes into account a range of factors. If it is decided that you do not have main responsibility for a child, you will not be treated as a lone parent. This means you will not be entitled to additional amounts for a child, you will be subject to the work-related requirements that apply to your other circumstances, and the amount you can get for rent may be reduced if you have a spare bedroom for a child to stay with you.

Box A

Lone parents and looking for work

Your 'work-related requirements' depend on the age of your youngest child.

- If you have a child under the age of one, you have no work-related requirements, so you can look after your new baby and get universal credit without having to worry about work during the first year.

- If you have a child aged one to four, you must attend 'work-focused interviews', usually every six months, to discuss your employability.

- Once your youngest child turns five, you are subject to all work-related requirements, which means you must look for work and be available to take up a job. You are allowed to place some restrictions on the type of work and the hours you are prepared to do.

- As long as you have a child aged under 13, you are allowed to limit your expected hours of work to fit in with your child's normal school hours including travel, so you only need to be available for work while s/he is at school. Most people are required to attend an interview or take up a job immediately, but as a lone parent, you may be allowed up to one month's notice to take up work or 48 hours' to attend an interview, taking into account how long you need to arrange childcare.

- From 2015, you are likely to be required to prepare for work once your youngest child has turned three.

If you do not comply with your work-related requirements, your universal credit may be 'sanctioned' and you will receive a reduced amount. If you are sanctioned, 'hardship payments' may be available. There is more information about sanctions in Chapter 6.

There are exceptions to work-related requirements if you have experienced domestic violence within the previous six months.

Childcare is a crucial consideration for most lone parents when contemplating taking up work. The availability of childcare support has been extended under universal credit. There is no minimum number of hours you must work to qualify for help with childcare; any work can qualify as long as the amount of childcare is not considered excessive in relation to how many hours you work. Universal credit may include an amount to help with childcare costs if you are paying a registered childcare provider such as a childminder, nursery or after-school club. The full costs of your childcare are not covered – only 70 per cent of the costs, up to a maximum payment of £532 a month for one child or £910 for two or more children. You can claim childcare costs before starting work if you have been offered a job that is due to start the following month, to allow a settling-in period for your child. Childcare costs can include deposits or up-front fees, but remember that universal credit is paid in arrears. You cannot claim for an amount that is paid or reimbursed by your employer or someone else, or covered by other support. You can continue to claim childcare costs for up to a month after stopping work, to allow you to find another job without losing the childcare place. You must report your actual childcare costs on a monthly basis; if they are not reported by the end of the following month, they cannot be met. It is your responsibility to report childcare costs, not the childcare provider's, although they may be required to confirm the costs. There is no system of automatic notification as with earnings.

What about other benefits for lone parents?

Child benefit remains outside universal credit, and is administered by HM Revenue and Customs. You should claim child benefit for your children as well as universal credit. You do not have to claim child benefit to prove that you are responsible for the child for universal credit.

Lone parents who have been bereaved can still claim widowed parent's allowance. You may be entitled to widowed parent's allowance at the same time as universal credit, but you cannot get both in full. Widowed parent's allowance and widow's pension count as unearned income for universal credit and the amount is deducted in full from your universal credit. The government has proposed separate reforms to bereavement benefits, which include an option to limit payments to one year.

You can get a Sure Start maternity grant if you get universal credit. This is £500 to help with the costs of a new baby, but it is usually only payable for your first child. It does not matter about other income or whether you are in work, as long as you are entitled to universal credit.

If you are pregnant or have a child under four, and you get universal credit, you should telephone the Healthy Start helpline (0845 607 6823) to ask about Healthy Start vouchers for milk, fruit and vegetables, and free vitamins.

The 'job grant' and 'in-work credit' for lone parents are being abolished. It is no longer possible to qualify for these payments from 1 April 2013 and 1 October 2013 respectively.

EXAMPLE

Lone parent

Martha is a lone parent with one child aged six. She gets universal credit and must be actively seeking and available for work. Her claimant commitment allows her to restrict her availability for work to school hours during term-time only. She is asked to attend a skills assessment course for two weeks while her child is at school. If she refuses to go, she is likely to be sanctioned. She is offered a temporary job of four hours a day during school hours, three days a week. If she does not accept the job, she may be sanctioned. The job continues to be available during the school holidays. Martha can get help with 70 per cent of childcare costs through universal credit, so she can continue working. If suitable childcare is not available, she should not be sanctioned for giving up the job.

2. Carers

Can carers claim universal credit?

Carers looking after a severely disabled person can claim universal credit. You are a carer if you have caring responsibilities for a severely disabled person, and you are not paid to provide care. To be recognised as severely disabled, the person you look after must get disability living allowance at the middle or highest rate for care, personal independence payment for daily living (either rate) or attendance allowance (either rate). You may be recognised as a carer for universal credit even if you do not get carer's allowance.

Are there any special rules for carers?

There is an additional amount in universal credit for people who have regular and substantial caring responsibilities for a severely disabled person. This means that you provide care for at least 35 hours a week.

You can get the additional amount as a carer whether or not you have made a claim for carer's allowance (but not if someone else gets carer's allowance for the same person). If more than one person has regular and substantial caring responsibilities for the same disabled person, the carer addition can only be paid for one of them. If you are in a couple and you are both carers, you can get two carer additions, but you must be looking after different people. If you both look after the same person, you should decide who is the main carer or the DWP will decide for you, and the other partner will usually have to look for work.

The carer's addition is not payable at the same time as a 'limited capability for work' or 'limited capability for work-related activity' addition for yourself if you are also disabled. So this means that if you are a disabled carer, you should make this clear in your claim and the DWP must award the amount of the highest value. If you are in a couple, you can get a carer's addition for yourself and a limited capability for work or limited capability for work-related activity addition for your disabled partner.

Carers who are in work have their overall universal credit award reduced, in the same way as other claimants. There is no extra work allowance for carers. However, you do not lose the carer's addition in universal credit just because you are working (even if you earn more than the £100 a week limit for carer's allowance), provided you are still caring for at least 35 hours a week.

Carers who spend at least 35 hours a week caring for a severely disabled person do not have any work-related requirements, so you can get universal credit without being expected to look for work. There may also be no work-related requirements if:

- you care for more than one severely disabled person and your total caring responsibilities are at least 35 hours a week
- you care for a severely disabled person for at least 35 hours a week, but you are not the main carer, perhaps because someone else gets carer's allowance for looking after her/him

In these cases, the decision maker must be satisfied that it is unreasonable to expect you to look for work, even within agreed limits. However, you do not get the additional amount as a carer in these cases.

If you spend less than 35 hours a week caring, or you care for a disabled person who does not get disability living allowance at the middle or highest rate for care, personal independence payment for daily living or attendance allowance, you are expected to look for work, within limits if agreed in your claimant commitment. You can restrict the hours you are available and looking for work so that this is compatible with your caring responsibilities, as long as this is agreed and you still have a reasonable chance of finding work. This may also apply if the disabled person is waiting to hear about a new claim for personal independence payment or attendance allowance – but there is no rule that automatically treats you as a carer while the claim is being decided, so any flexibility in your work-related requirements must be agreed in your claimant commitment.

If you are a foster carer (or approved kinship carer in Scotland), see Box B.

What about other benefits for carers?

Carers can still claim carer's allowance. You must spend at least 35 hours a week looking after a severely disabled person who gets disability living allowance at the middle or higher rate for care, personal independence payment for daily living (either rate) or attendance allowance (either rate). You cannot get carer's allowance if you are a full-time student or earning over £100 a week. Carer's allowance counts as income in full for universal credit. However, it is not enough to live on, so you may get a top-up of universal credit as well. If you have claimed carer's allowance and meet the conditions but have been told that it cannot be paid because you get another benefit (such as contributory employment and support allowance), you can still be treated as a carer for universal credit. If you are earning over £100 a week, but you meet the other conditions for carer's allowance, you can still be treated as a carer for universal credit, even if you have not actually claimed carer's allowance.

Box B
Foster carers

- Foster carers who are legally approved to look after a child or young person by arrangement with a local authority or voluntary organisation are treated differently from carers looking after a disabled person.

- In Scotland, approved kinship carers are treated in the same way as foster carers.

- There are special rules for foster carers in universal credit.

- Lone foster carers are only required to attend work-focused interviews, and do not have any other 'work-related requirements' until their youngest foster child reaches 16, when they are required to look for and be available for work.

- In exceptional circumstances when a foster child who is 16 or 17 needs full-time care, the foster carer is only required to participate in 'work-focused interviews' until the child reaches 18 or the placement ends.

- Fostering couples must say which one of the couple is the lead carer. The lead carer is only required to attend work-focused interviews. The other member of the couple has all the 'work-related requirements' that apply to her/his circumstances, unless there are exceptional circumstances and the foster child needs full-time care by two adults.

- Fostering is not treated as being self-employed or in work.

- Fostering payments are not taken into account as earnings or income. There is no additional amount in universal credit for being a foster carer.

Carer

Duncan is a carer for his brother, who gets personal independence payment for daily living. Duncan gets universal credit and has no work-related requirements. His brother's personal independence payment stops following a review. Duncan no longer meets the conditions as a carer for a severely disabled person, so he becomes subject to all work-related requirements. He is able to agree some restrictions in his claimant commitment on his hours of availability for work and the notice required to attend an interview or take up a job. His personal adviser must be satisfied that his brother still has a physical or mental impairment. Duncan is still required to show that he is taking all reasonable action to find work within the agreed restrictions, or he may be sanctioned.

3. Disabled people

Can disabled people claim universal credit?

People with disabilities can claim universal credit. The amount that you get and the conditions that you have to meet depend on the extent of your disability, as assessed by the DWP.

Are there any special rules for disabled people?

There are special rules for some people with disabilities. These affect how much universal credit you get, what kind of 'work-related requirements' you have and, if you work, how much of your earnings you can keep before your universal credit is affected.

Universal credit can include additional amounts for disabled adults and children. The amounts are the same for adults and children and are paid at either of two rates, depending on the severity of the disability, but the criteria are different for adults and children.

For a child, this depends on the amount of disability living allowance or personal independence payment s/he gets. This is explained in Chapter 3.

For an adult, the additional amount depends on a medical assessment of your capability for work, as used for employment and support allowance. This is explained in Chapter 3.

The additional amount for adults is not related to disability living allowance or personal independence payment, and it does not make any difference whether you live alone or have a carer. For a couple, there is only one additional amount, even if both partners are sick or disabled.

If you are disabled and you also care for someone who is disabled, you cannot get a limited capability for work or work-related activity addition as well as a carer's addition for yourself in universal credit. However, if you are in a couple and you are disabled and your partner is a carer, you could get a limited capability for work or work-related activity addition for yourself and a carer's addition for your partner.

Disabled people are allowed to earn more than some other claimants before their universal credit is reduced. There is a 'work allowance' for disabled people, including couples where either partner is disabled. This is the amount you can earn before your universal credit is reduced. You qualify for this disregard if you or your partner have been assessed as having limited capability for work.

If you are a disabled person getting universal credit and you start work, you do not automatically stop having limited capability for work, so you do not necessarily lose the additional amount and work allowance, but your capability for work may be reassessed. If you are a disabled person in work and your weekly earnings are equal to 16 times the national minimum wage or higher, you can only be newly assessed as having limited capability for work to get the additional amount or higher work allowance if you get disability living allowance or personal independence payment.

What about other benefits for disabled people?

You can still claim contributory employment and support allowance if you have worked and paid enough national insurance contributions, although payment is limited to one year for most people. You may be entitled to contributory employment and support allowance at the same time as universal credit, but you cannot receive both in full. Contributory employment and support allowance counts as income in full for universal credit, so it reduces your entitlement. In some situations, you can get contributory employment and support allowance if you cannot get universal credit – eg, if your savings are too high.

If you are entitled to contributory employment and support allowance and universal credit, or you move from one to another, the rules on 'work-related requirements', 'sanctions' and 'hardship payments' apply to both benefits.

Disability living allowance is being abolished and replaced by personal independence payment for working-age claimants. You can continue to receive disability living allowance or personal independence payment, as these remain outside universal credit and do not count as income.

The 'job grant' and 'return-to-work credit' for sick or disabled people are being abolished. It is no longer possible to qualify for these payments from 1 April 2013 and 1 October 2013 respectively.

EXAMPLE

Disabled person

Sarah is a single person who has previously been in good health, working 20 hours a week on the minimum wage. She gets universal credit, but is expected to look for better paid work or more hours. She is diagnosed with a long-term health condition and feels that this is affecting her ability to work. She does not want to give up her job, but feels that she should be entitled to additional support through universal credit as a disabled worker. She asks to be assessed for limited capability for work, which would allow her more to live on, allow more of her earnings to be ignored, and she would not have to be actively seeking more work. Her request is refused because she is already working more than 16 hours a week. She must first apply for personal independence payment – if this is awarded, she can then be assessed for limited capability for work in universal credit.

4. Older people

Can older people claim universal credit?

Older people cannot usually claim universal credit. One of the basic qualifying conditions is that you have not reached the qualifying age for pension credit, but there is an exception for couples.

The qualifying age for pension credit for men and women is around 61 years and nine months in October 2013, when universal credit is introduced, but is gradually rising to 65 by November 2018, and to 66 by October 2020.

- Single people over the qualifying age for pension credit cannot claim universal credit.

- Couples who are both over the qualifying age for pension credit cannot claim universal credit.

- A couple with one partner who has reached the qualifying age for pension credit and one under the qualifying age for pension credit can claim universal credit, but cannot claim pension credit. Couples who are already on pension credit when universal credit is introduced can remain on pension credit.

A couple where one is over pension credit qualifying age are entitled to universal credit as joint claimants. The older person's income and capital is included. The older person must share responsibility for the claim and accept a claimant commitment, but is not required to look for work.

Are there any special rules for older people?

There is no additional amount for older people in universal credit. This means that a couple on universal credit, where one is over pension credit qualifying age, actually receive less than a single person on pension credit.

If a couple is claiming universal credit, only the working-age partner has 'work-related requirements'. However, if the working-age partner fails to meet her/his requirements, the couple may still be 'sanctioned', which means losing half of their universal credit standard allowance for a period of time.

What about other benefits for older people?

Universal credit does not replace pension credit or retirement pension. You cannot get pension credit and universal credit at the same time. You may be entitled to one but not the other, but you do not have a choice about which one to claim. Pension credit is changing to include additional amounts for rent and for children, following the abolition of housing benefit and child tax credit. Housing benefit for people over the qualifying age for pension credit will remain until October 2014, when it is due to be replaced by the new addition in pension credit for rent. It is expected that tax credit claims from most new claimants are not accepted from 6 April 2014, but older people can still claim child tax credit after this date if they are responsible for children, until a new amount is included in pension credit for children. If you get retirement pension and your partner is under pension credit qualifying age, you can get universal credit, but retirement pension is counted as income in full.

There are separate plans to reform state retirement pension. Attendance allowance and the winter fuel payment remain outside universal credit and are not counted as income.

EXAMPLE

Older couple

Sanjay and Geeta are a couple who have both recently lost their jobs and get universal credit. Sanjay is aged 62; he reaches the qualifying age for pension credit after universal credit is introduced in their area. Geeta is aged 58. They cannot make a new claim for pension credit as a couple, and continue to be entitled to universal credit. They do not get any extra money now that Sanjay is over pension credit qualifying age. It is a joint claim, but it is only Geeta who must look for work. She fails to apply for a sufficient number of jobs and is sanctioned, which means losing half of their couple allowance, so that they are left with about £240 a month to live on. This is putting a strain on their relationship, and Sanjay has heard that he would get more than double this amount if they split up and he claimed pension credit as a single person.

5. People from abroad

Can people from abroad claim universal credit?

People who have come to live in the UK from other countries can claim universal credit if they have certain types of permission to live in the UK, but some groups are excluded. One of the basic conditions for universal credit is that you must be in Great Britain – see Chapter 2 for more information.

You can get universal credit if you are a national of a European Economic Area country, although you are subject to special rules which usually mean that you or a family member must be working in the UK, or you are looking for work. There are additional restrictions on nationals of Bulgaria, Romania and Croatia, which usually mean you must be in certain types of work, or self-employed.

If you are from a country outside the European Economic Area, you can get universal credit if you can stay in the UK indefinately without restrictions. You can also get universal credit if the UK government has recognised you as a refugee, or granted you humanitarian protection or exceptional leave to enter or remain in the UK.

'Persons subject to immigration control' are excluded from universal credit. This means you cannot get universal credit if your entry clearance to the UK says that you must have 'no recourse to public funds'. This is usually stamped in your passport if you are from outside the European Economic Area and you are in the UK as a student, visitor or with a work visa. Universal credit counts as 'public funds'.

You cannot get universal credit if you are an asylum seeker. You are an asylum seeker if you are waiting for a decision from the Home Office on an application for refugee status in the UK, or if you are appealing against a negative decision. The asylum support system is run by the Home Office and is outside universal credit.

If only your partner is subject to immigration control, you can claim universal credit as a single person, for yourself and any children and housing costs, but your partner's income and capital is still taken into account.

Are there any special rules for people from abroad?

You are not entitled to universal credit if you are not 'habitually resident' in the UK. This includes showing that you are settled in the UK, usually having been in the UK for one to three months, and also applies to British citizens returning to the UK from living abroad.

You may be excluded from universal credit if you do not have the 'right to reside' in the UK. This particularly affects you if you are a national of a European Economic Area country. You are generally required to show a link to the labour market as a worker, self-employed person, jobseeker or family member.

If you are a European Economic Area national and your only right to reside is as a jobseeker or a family member of a jobseeker, you must look for work, as described in Chapter 5. In this case, even if you are a lone parent with a child under five, a carer or you have limited capability for work, you are still subject to all work-related requirements.

What about other benefits for people from abroad?

There are special rules for certain groups of people from abroad for most of the other benefits.

EXAMPLE

Person from abroad

Mika is a European Economic Area national who came to the UK to look for work. She is entitled to universal credit and is subject to all work-related requirements. Before she is able to find work, she finds out she is pregnant. After the baby is born, she thought she would only have to attend work-focused interviews as a lone parent with a child under the age of five. However, as her only right to reside in the UK is as a jobseeker, she is still subject to all work-related requirements. If she stops looking for work, she does not have a right to reside and is not entitled to universal credit at all.

---

6. Young people

Can young people claim universal credit?

One of the basic conditions for universal credit is that you must be aged at least 18 to claim. However, there are special rules that allow some young people aged 16 and 17 to claim universal credit. If you are aged under 16, you cannot claim universal credit in any circumstances; a responsible adult who you live with should claim for you, or the local authority must have responsibility for you.

Are there any special rules for young people?

If you are aged 16 or 17, you can claim universal credit for yourself, and any housing costs you are liable for and any children you are responsible for if you:

- have a child or are about to have a baby
- are 'without parental support'
- are disabled or ill
- are a carer

Chapter 2 explains more about when you can claim in these situations.

If you are a care leaver aged 16 or 17, you cannot usually get universal credit and the local authority still has a duty to support you. You can only get universal credit as a care leaver if you are disabled or responsible for a child.

Young people may also be affected by the basic condition for universal credit that you must not be receiving education, although there are some exceptions which are explained in Chapter 2.

Young people under the age of 25 are entitled to less universal credit than people aged 25 and over.

What about other benefits for young people?

There are not many other benefits that young people aged 16 or 17 can claim for themselves. If you are disabled, you may be able to claim personal independence payment. If you are a carer, you may be able to claim carer's allowance. You can only claim contributory benefits such as employment and support allowance or jobseeker's allowance if you have worked and paid enough national insurance contributions, usually for two to three years before you claim.

EXAMPLE

Young person estranged from parents

Zoe is aged 17 and has recently left school and started work. She has an argument with her parents and leaves home. She finds a room in private rented accommodation, and claims universal credit. She is below the normal qualifying age of 18, and has to make statement explaining that she is estranged from her parents. The decision maker looks at her statement and the guidance which says there is no requirement to corroborate such evidence or contact parents. Zoe should be believed unless her statement is self-contradictory or improbable.

Further information

There is more information about the rules for current benefits and tax credits in CPAG's *Welfare benefits and Tax Credits Handbook*.

Appendix 1

Glossary of terms

Actively looking for work
Looking for paid work. A person must normally spend the same number of hours a week looking for work as the Department for Work and Pensions expects her/him to work.

Alternative payment arrangements
Discretion to pay universal credit twice a month, directly to a landlord or split between partners.

Appointee
Someone, usually a relative, who is authorised by the Department for Work and Pensions to claim benefit on another person's behalf if that person cannot claim for her/himself – eg, perhaps because of a learning disability.

Assessment period
The monthly period on which your universal credit payment is based. You are paid up to seven days after the end of each assessment period.

Available for work
Willing and able to take up work. This normally means immediately able to start full-time work, but may be restricted if the Department for Work and Pensions agrees it is reasonable.

Benefit cap
The maximum amount of social security benefits that someone can receive. This includes most benefits, but there are some exceptions and some groups to whom the cap does not apply.

Capital
This includes savings, investments, certain lump-sum payments and property which is not a person's main home.

Civil penalty
A fine that can be imposed if someone is overpaid a benefit because s/he failed to provide information or gave incorrect information, and is not being prosecuted for fraud or another benefit offence.

Claimant commitment

A document setting out what someone must do while claiming universal credit, and the possible penalties if its terms are not met.

Contributory benefit

A benefit for which entitlement depends on having paid a certain amount of national insurance contributions.

Couple

A man and a woman (or two people of the same sex) living together who are married or civil partners, or who are living together as if they were married or civil partners.

Earnings threshold

The amount of a person's earnings (or joint earnings for couples) above which s/he is not expected to look for more work, or meet any other work-related requirements.

Elements

Amounts for children, disabilities, caring responsibilities, housing and childcare which make up part of a person's maximum universal credit award.

European Economic Area

The 28 European Union member states, plus Iceland, Norway and Liechtenstein. For benefit purposes, Switzerland is also treated as part of the European Economic Area.

Habitually resident

Someone who has a settled intention to stay in the UK, and who has usually been living here for a period.

Hardship payments

Payments of universal credit made if someone's entitlement has been reduced by a sanction and s/he faces financial hardship. These are loans and must be paid back.

Independent Case Examiner

A body handling complaints against the Department for Work and Pensions.

Judicial review
A way of challenging the decisions of government departments, local authorities and some tribunals against which there is no right of appeal.

Limited capability for work
A test of whether a person's ability to work is limited by a health condition.

Limited capability for work-related activity
A test of how severe a person's health problems are and whether her/his ability to prepare for work is limited.

Means-tested benefit
A benefit that is only paid if someone's income and capital are low enough.

National minimum wage
A set minimum hourly rate that employers must pay.

No recourse to public funds
A restriction that applies to people subject to immigration control as part of their entry conditions to the UK, prohibiting them from claiming most benefits and tax credits, including universal credit.

Non-contributory benefit
A benefit for which entitlement does not depend on having paid a certain amount of national insurance contributions.

Non-means-tested benefit
A benefit that is paid regardless of the amount of someone's income or capital.

Overpayment
An amount of benefit or tax credits that is paid which is more than a person's entitlement.

Passporting
A term used to describe when entitlement to a particular benefit allows access to other benefits or sources of help.

Payment on account
An advance of universal credit, paid if there is a delay in deciding someone's claim or in cases of financial need.

Penalty as an alternative to prosecution
A type of fine that can be offered to someone instead of being prosecuted, if the Department for Work and Pensions thinks an offence may have been committed.

Person subject to immigration control
Someone who requires leave to enter or remain in the UK but does not have it, or who has leave to remain but is prohibited from having recourse to public funds, or has leave to remain in the UK on the basis of a sponsorship agreement.

Personal adviser
A person whose job is to discuss your work-related requirements. S/he may be an employee of the Department for Work and Pensions, or someone contracted to provide services under the Work Programme.

Qualifying age for pension credit
Linked to women's pension age, which is currently increasing from age 60, will equalise with men's pension age in 2018 and will reach 66 in 2020.

Real-time information system
A new system where employers send HM Revenue and Customs information about employees' earnings every time they are paid, which is then used by the Department for Work and Pensions to adjust universal credit awards.

Responsible carer
The person in a couple who spends the most time looking after the children. Must be jointly nominated by the couple.

Revision
A statutory method that allows benefit decisions to be changed.

Right to reside
A social security test, mainly affecting European Economic Area nationals, which must be satisfied in order to claim certain benefits.

Sanction
A reduction in a person's universal credit award for failing to meet her/his work-related requirements without a good reason. The term is also used if a person's universal credit is stopped for a set length of time because s/he has committed an offence.

Standard allowance
The basic amount of universal credit paid for a single adult or a couple.

Supersession
A statutory method which allows benefit decisions to be changed, usually as a result of a change in circumstances.

Taper
The rate at which a person's maximum universal credit will reduce as her/his earnings increase.

Transitional protection
A way of making sure that a person transferring to universal credit from another benefit will not receive less money on universal credit than s/he did before.

Waiting period
The time at the start of a benefit claim before payment can start, or before payment of housing costs or limited capability for work/work-related activity element can start.

Work allowance
The amount of a person's wages or income from self-employment that can be kept before her/his universal credit starts being reduced. The amount depends on personal circumstances.

Work preparation
The activities that someone may have to undertake to prepare for a future return to work, such as increasing skills or doing work placements.

Work-focused interview
An interview to discuss future work opportunities and the barriers that may prevent someone from working.

Work-focused health-related assessment

An assessment of the barriers to working caused by a person's health problems or disability, which may have to be carried out if s/he is required to prepare for work.

Work-related requirements

The activities that a person must undertake to continue to receive the full amount of universal credit.

Index